Step-by-Step
Classic Recipes

igloobooks
.com

Published in 2012
by Igloo Books Ltd
Cottage Farm
Sywell
Northants
NN6 0BJ
www.igloobooks.com

Copyright © 2012 Igloo Books Ltd

Food photography and recipe development: PhotoCuisine UK
Front and back cover images © PhotoCuisine UK

HUN001 0812
2 4 6 8 10 9 7 5 3 1
ISBN: 978-0-85780-733-5

Printed and manufactured in China

Step-by-Step
Classic Recipes

Contents

Stuffed Peppers

Ingredients

Peppers:

6 small bell peppers

250 g / 9 oz / 2 cups bulgur

4 tomatoes

2 onions

1 tsp of cumin

Yoghurt sauce:

2 Bulgarian yoghurts

2 tsp of olive oil

2 tsp of mustard

mint leaves or chives

lemon, salt, pepper, nutmeg, paprika

SERVES 4 | PREP TIME 20 minutes | COOKING TIME 20 minutes

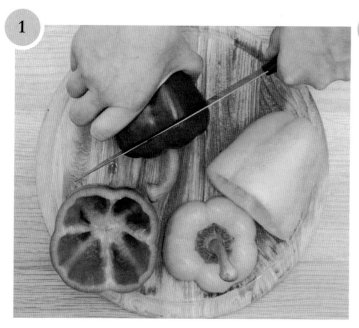

Slice the top off of the peppers and reserve to one side.

Cook the bulgur in salted boiling water for 20 minutes.

3

Chop the onion and the tomatoes into small cubes.

4

De-seed all of the peppers and slice just 2 of them into cubes.

5

Place in a pan. Add the bulgur, salt and pepper, a little cumin and cook for 10 minutes over medium heat.

6

7

Cook the remaining 4 peppers in a steamer for 10 minutes. Meanwhile, prepare the yoghurt sauce by mixing all of the ingredients together.

Once cooked, stuff the peppers with the bulgur mixture.

8

Top the peppers with the yoghurt sauce. Place the tops of the peppers back in place and serve warm.

Mushroom Soup

Ingredients

10 large mushrooms and 10 small ones for
topping
100 g / 4 oz / 1 cup cheddar cheese
1 onion
20 g / ⅔ oz / ⅙ stick of butter
200 ml / 7 fl. oz / ⅘ crème fraiche
100 ml / 3 ½ fl. oz / ⅖ milk
salt and pepper

SERVES 4 | PREP TIME 10 minutes | COOKING TIME 25 minutes

Prepare and measure all of the ingredients. Grate the cheese.

2

Wash the large mushrooms and cut into large chunks.

3

Peel and cut the onion into thin slices.

4

In a saucepan, brown the onion in half of the butter for 1 minute. Add the mushrooms and cook 5 minutes.

5

Cover with water and cook for 15 minutes on a medium heat.

6

Add the crème fraiche, season and mix with a food processor. In another saucepan, boil the milk, cream and cheese.

7

Season with salt and pepper and blend well. Add the mixture to the soup.

8

Slice the small mushrooms thinly and fry in a pan with the rest of the butter. Season with salt and pepper. Serve the soup topped with the mushrooms.

Chicken Nuggets

Ingredients

8 chicken breasts

450 ml / 16 fl. oz / 1 ⅘ cups of milk

150 g / 5 oz / 1 cup of plain (all-purpose)
flour

225 g / 8 oz / 2 cups of breadcrumbs

3 eggs

salt and pepper

SERVES 6 | PREP TIME 20 minutes | COOKING TIME 20 minutes

The day before, put the chicken breasts in a bowl, cover with milk, and place the bowl in the fridge overnight.

On the day, preheat the oven to 180°C (160° fan) / 350F / gas 4. Drain the chicken pieces and place them on a tray.

Season the pieces with salt and pepper on both sides.

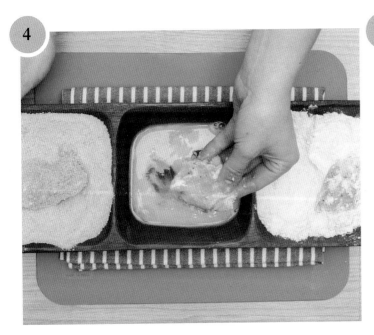

Put the flour and breadcrumbs in 2 different bowls and beat the eggs in a third. Roll each piece of chicken in the flour, then in the beaten egg and finally in the breadcrumbs.

Arrange on a baking tray covered with baking paper, not touching. Cook the nuggets for 10 minutes on each side, until they are golden. Serve with a salad or green vegetables, and your choice of dip.

Minestrone

Ingredients

For the soup

150 g / 5 oz / 1 cup of short macaroni

100 g / 4 oz / 1 cup of grated Parmesan

2 tomatoes

2 carrots

2 courgettes

1 leek

2 cubes of beef stock

2 cloves of garlic

¼ ball of celeriac

100 g / 4 oz / ½ cup dried beans

1 bouquet garni (parsley, thyme, bay leaves)

12 basil leaves

4 tsp of olive oil

1.5 l / 3 pints of water

salt and pepper

SERVES 4 | PREP TIME 20 minutes | COOKING TIME 90 minutes

The night before, soak the beans in a bowl of cold water. The next day, put them in a saucepan, cover with water and cook for 30 minutes then drain.

Boil the water and add the stock cubes to it. Peel the carrots, potato, leek and celeriac, wash them as well as the courgettes. Plunge the tomatoes quickly in a pan of boiling water and then peel and seed them.

Cut all the vegetables into cubes. Peel the garlic and crush it. Preheat the oven to 120°C (100° fan) / 240F / gas 2.

Sauté all the vegetables in a pan over a medium heat for 5 minutes. Then transfer to a baking dish and add the beans, garlic, basil and bouquet garni.

Add the stock and season with salt and pepper. Leave it to simmer on a low heat for 40 minutes. Ten minutes before the end of cooking, add the macaroni. Serve in a deep bowl, with grated Parmesan.

Chicken Liver Pâté

Ingredients

250 g / 9 oz chicken livers

60 ml / 2 fl. oz / ¼ cup of brandy

500 g / 1 lb 2 oz minced pork

150 g / 5 oz of pork rind/lard

1 bouquet garni : thyme and bay leaf

salt and pepper

SERVES 6-8 | PREP TIME 30 minutes | COOKING TIME 60 minutes

Put the livers in a bowl with the thyme and bay leaf. Pour over the brandy. If possible, marinate a few hours. It is not compulsory to marinate, but it brings out the taste.

Chop the livers, except for two that you will leave full. Mix the minced meat, liver and brandy and season with salt and pepper.

Preheat the oven at 160°C (140° fan) / 300F / gas 2. Line a loaf tin with the rind.

Fill with the minced meat and incorporate the chopped livers gradually for texture.

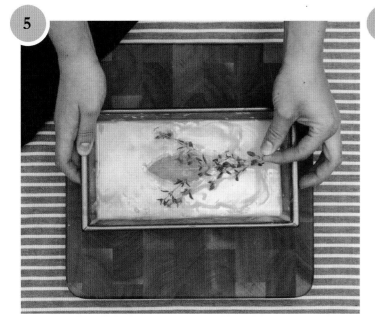

Put the bouquet garni and pork rind on top, to protect the top of the pate.

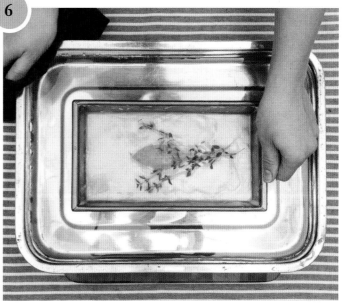

Place the dish in a bigger dish containing cold water and cover with foil. Cook for 1 hour. Let it cool completely. The pâté can be kept in the fridge for a few days.

Tomato Soup

Ingredients

1 kg / 2 lb 4 oz of tomatoes

1 onion

2 cloves garlic

handful of fresh basil leaves

1 tbsp extra virgin olive oil

2 tbsp single cream

salt and pepper

SERVES 4 | PREP TIME 15 minutes | COOKING TIME 20 minutes

Prepare and measure all of the ingredients. Peel and chop the onion and garlic.

Sauté the onion and garlic in a pan with 1 tbsp of olive oil, for 2 minutes.

Wash the tomatoes and cut them into small pieces. Put the tomato pieces into a pan of water, bring to the boil and then gently simmer for 15 minutes. Season with salt and pepper.

Add the onion, basil and garlic and mix together in a bowl. Place in a food processor and blend well.

For consistency, pass the mixture through a sieve and then place in a saucepan. Add the cream and gently heat for a few minutes.

Serve into warm bowls and decorate with a couple of basil leaves.

Potato Boats

Ingredients

4 large Potatoes

30 g / 1 oz / ¼ stick of butter

110 g / 4 oz / 1 cup cheddar cheese

8 slices of bacon, crumbled

120 ml / 4 fl. oz / ½ cup of milk

120 ml / 4 fl. oz / ½ cup soft cheese

olive oil for brushing

salt and pepper

SERVES 4 | PREP TIME 15 minutes | COOKING TIME 90 minutes

1 Pre heat the oven to 180°C (160° fan) / 350F / gas 4. Wash and prick the potatoes using a fork.

2 Brush the potatoes with oil and sprinkle salt on the skin. Then cook on a baking tray for 50 minutes until the potatoes are tender.

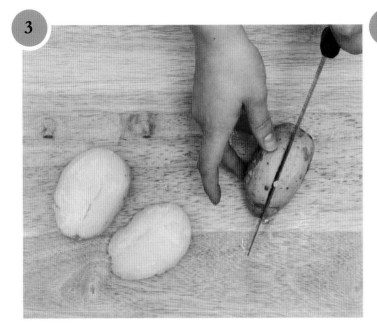

Once cooked, slice the potatoes in half, lengthwise and scoop out some of the middle.

Place the scooped out middle into a bowl, mix with the butter and the soft cheese.

Add the bacon and half of the cheddar and stir.

Add the milk and stir until the mixture is smooth. Stuff the potato skins with the mixture. Bake for 30 minutes. Add the remaining cheese in the last 5 minutes and serve warm.

Pan-fried Scallops

Ingredients

6 scallops per person

dozen small leeks

2 onions

250 ml / 9 fl. oz / 1 cup of white wine (dry)

150 ml / 5 fl. oz / ⅔ fish stock

bouquet garni (thyme and bay leaf)

salted butter for cooking

salt and pepper

SERVES 6-8 | PREP TIME 20 minutes | COOKING TIME 40 minutes

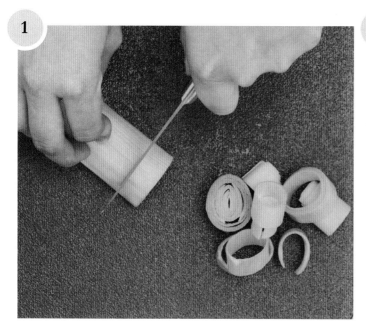

Chop the leeks in 1 cm / ½ inch slices.

Reserve one leek and cut vertically in long strings for decoration.

3

Cook the leeks over medium heat in butter and fish stock.

4

Add 1 or 2 onions, chopped into small pieces. Add the white wine, salt, pepper and bouquet garni.

5

Cook for 15 minutes, until the leeks are cooked but not pureed.

6

Remove from the heat and reserve with some of the cooking juice. Cook the scallops in fish stock for 10 minutes.

7

Next, brown the scallops quickly in some butter.

8

Serve the leeks in a deep plate, covered with the scallops and decorated with the long pieces of leek. Pour some of the cooking juice over the scallops.

Calamari

Ingredients

1 kg / 2 lb 4oz white calamari (squid)

1 l / 1 pt 16 fl. oz / 4 cups vegetable oil

5 pinches of coarse salt

200 g / 7 oz / 1 ⅓ cup of wheat flour

5 g / ¼ oz of baking powder

200 ml / 7 fl. oz / ⅘ cup of sparkling water

1 lemon

SERVES 6 | PREP TIME 15 minutes | COOKING TIME 20 minutes

Prepare the squid by removing the skin, eyes and insides.

Clean with running water, and then cut the squid into thin rings 1 cm / ½ inch thick.

3

In a bowl, mix ¾ of the flour, the baking powder and salt.

4

Add cold water and mix gently with a whisk (to obtain crispy fritters, use sparkling water).

5

Heat frying oil to 180°C / 350F. Place the sliced squid in the remaining ¼ of the flour, then into the batter.

6

Dip them in hot cooking oil until golden brown (don't pace too many at one time otherwise they will stick together).

7

Once browned, drain the fried Calamaries on a paper towel.

8

Taste and season with salt. Slice the lemon in wedges. Serve hot immediately with accompanying salad and lemon wedges.

Breaded Camembert

Ingredients

250 g / 9 oz wheel of Camembert

60 g / 2 oz / ⅓ cup plain (all-purpose) flour

2 eggs

1 tbsp of Brandy

pinch grated nutmeg

50 g / 2 oz readymade bread crumbs

vegetable oil for cooking

salt and pepper

SERVES 4 | PREP TIME 15 minutes | COOKING TIME 5 minutes

Scrape the thick coat of crumb from the camembert.

Cut into triangle pieces and place to one side. Put the flour on a plate.

3

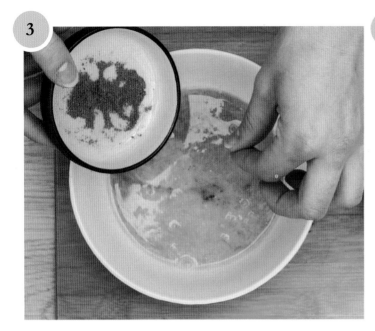

Beat the eggs in a bowl. Add the nutmeg and Brandy.

4

Place the breadcrumbs on a plate. Roll each piece of Camembert in the flour and then the egg mixture.

5

Next, roll each piece in the breadcrumbs and set to one side.

6

Heat the oil in a pan. When the oil is hot, place the Camembert pieces in the pan and turn on all sides until golden. Serve with green salad and toasts.

Salmon with Scrambled Eggs

Ingredients

350 g / 12 oz of smoked salmon

12 eggs

100 g / 3 ½ oz / 1 stick of butter

100 ml / 3 ½ fl. oz / ⅖ cup cream

bunch of chives

salt and pepper

green salad and lemon for decoration

SERVES 6 | PREP TIME 20 minutes | COOKING TIME 10 minutes

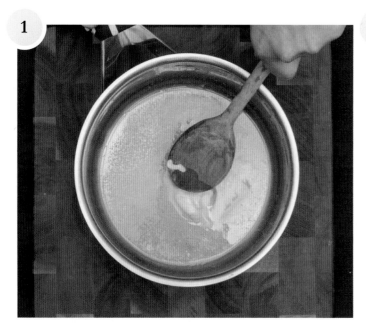

Pare the smoked salmon so that the slices are nice and regular. Melt the butter in a large saucepan over very low heat.

Rotate the pan so the butter coats the sides. Beat the eggs lightly with a fork and season with salt and pepper.

Pour them into the pan and allow them to thicken, whisking until all the egg mixture is cooked but still soft.

Remove from the heat, add the chopped chives.

Stir in the cream and blend gently using a wooden spoon.

Place the egg mixture on the smoked salmon slices then roll the slices and place on a serving plate with green salad and a wedge of lemon.

Brie Wedges

Ingredients

1 pack of brie
50 g / 2 oz / ⅓ cup flour
100 g / 4 oz / 1 cup breadcrumbs
2 eggs
vegetable oil for frying

For the redcurrant sauce:

2 tbsp redcurrant jam
1 tbsp balsamic vinegar

For the honey sauce:

2 tbsp liquid honey
1 tsp vinegar
1 tbsp grainy mustard

SERVES 2 | PREP TIME 15 minutes | COOKING TIME 5 minutes

In a bowl break and beat the eggs.

Place the flour and the breadcrumbs onto two separate plates.

Cut the brie into medium slices, 2 to 3 per person. Roll the slices in flour, then in the beaten eggs and finally the breadcrumbs.

Brown the pieces in a little hot oil, or deep fry them for a few minutes until just golden.

Prepare the redcurrant sauce by mixing the jam and balsamic vinegar together.

To make the honey sauce, mix the honey, mustard and vinegar together. Present the breaded Brie on a plate, accompanied by the two sauces.

Breaded Mushrooms

Ingredients

500 g / 1 lb button mushrooms, not too big

50 g / 2 oz / ⅓ cup flour, seasoned with salt and pepper

2 eggs, beaten

150 g / 5 oz / 1 ½ cups breadcrumbs

vegetable oil for cooking

For the dipping sauce:

200 g / 7 oz Greek yoghurt

½ tbsp dried chili

1 clove of garlic

25 g / 1 oz mixed herbs

salt and black pepper

SERVES 4-6 | PREP TIME 15 minutes | COOKING TIME 5 minutes

Roll the mushrooms in flour until completely coated.

Dip the mushrooms into the egg and coat all over.

3

Roll the mushrooms in the breadcrumbs, shaking the excess off.

4

Heat the oil and fry the mushrooms until golden brown. Carefully remove with a slotted spoon and drain on a paper towel.

5

For the sauce, peel the garlic clove and place all ingredients in a food processor, season with salt and pepper and blend until smooth.

6

Serve the mushrooms on a plate and decorate with herbs, sliced onions or lemon wedges. Place the sauce in small bowl.

Waldorf Salad

Ingredients

45 ml / 3 tbsp mayonnaise

30 ml / 2 tbsp whole cream

½ tsp sugar

2 apples (1 green, 1 red)

1 stalk of celery

80 g / ⅓ cup chopped walnuts

250 g / 9 oz / 1 cup of white seedless grapes

romaine lettuce leaves, for decoration

salt and black pepper

SERVES 4 | PREP TIME 15 minutes

In a small bowl, using a whisk, combine mayonnaise, cream and sugar until the sauce is smooth and creamy. Season with salt and pepper and reserve.

Wash and cut the apples into small cubes (without peeling them).

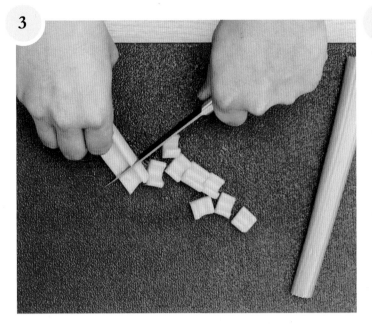

Wash and slice the celery into small chunks.

Halve the grapes and place in a small bowl.

Add the apples, celery chopped walnuts and mayonnaise sauce to the grapes.

Stir all of the ingredients together well to coat with all of the sauce. Serve salad on lettuce leaves and garnish with whole walnuts, if desired.

Roast Potatoes

Ingredients

900 g / 2 lb of medium sized new potatoes

3 tbsp olive oil

½ tsp Fleur de Sel

½ tsp freshly ground black pepper

3 large garlic cloves

1 tsp freshly chopped thyme

1 tsp freshly chopped flat leaf parsley

SERVES 4 | PREP TIME 10 minutes | COOKING TIME 60 minutes

Preheat the oven at 180°C (160° fan) / 350F / gas 4. Prepare and measure all of the ingredients.

Wash the potatoes and cut them into thick wedges, leaving the skin on.

In a large bowl combine the potatoes well with the olive oil, a pinch of salt, pepper and garlic.

Place into a roasting tray lined with foil.

Peel and crush the garlic and add to the tin. Bake for about 50 minutes while tossing regularly, until the potatoes are just golden.

Add the parsley and thyme and mix well with the potatoes. Bake for 10 more minutes. Serve with a couple of pinches of Fleur de Sel sprinkled over the top.

Caesar Salad

Ingredients

For the salad:

4 chicken breasts

cos green salad

100 g / 4 oz / 1 cup grated Parmesan

3 slices white toast bread, cut into small cubes

2 eggs

dash olive oil

1 lemon

1 shallot

chili powder

1 knob butter

salt and pepper

For the dressing:

4 tbsp sour cream

lemon juice

mustard

1 tbsp grated Parmesan cheese

1 tbsp balsamic vinegar

SERVES 4 | PREP TIME 4 hours | COOKING TIME 10 minutes

Pre-heat the oven at 200°C (180° fan) / 400F / gas 6. Place the bread cubes in a baking tray with a pinch of chilli powder and dash of olive oil. Bake for 10 minutes (until the croutons are golden brown) then remove from the oven and reserve.

Cook the 2 eggs in boiling water, until hard (10 minutes).

3

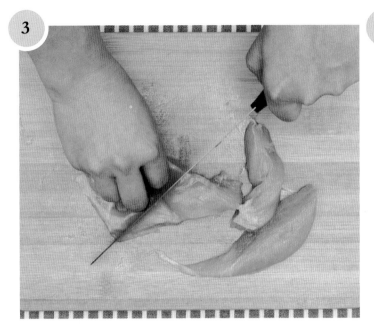

Slice the chicken breasts into thin slices and place in a separate dish.

4

Pour the juice of half the lemon over the chicken and leave it to marinate in the refrigerator for at least 4 hours.

5

Cook the marinated chicken breasts in a pan with the butter for 10 minutes, until fully cooked. Slice the chicken into 1 cm / ½ inch pieces.

6

Mix the salad, croutons, minced shallot, grated Parmesan and sliced chicken.

In a bowl, prepare the sauce with the Sour cream, mustard, lemon juice, some grated Parmesan and a little balsamic vinegar. Season with salt and pepper.

Pour the sauce over the chicken salad mix. Serve as an appetizer or main dish for a light meal. You can add anchovies to the recipe.

Shrimp Salad

Ingredients

24 king prawns (shrimps)

1 cos lettuce

For the Thousand Island dressing:

150 ml / 5 fl. oz mayonnaise

2 shallots

100 ml / 3 ½ fl. oz white wine

1 tbsp white wine vinegar

1 tsp mustard

2 tbsp tomato ketchup

1 tbsp of chopped tarragon

2 tsp of Brandy

4 drops of Worcestershire sauce

4 drops of Tabasco sauce

salt and pepper

SERVES 6 | PREP TIME 10 minutes | COOKING TIME 10 minutes

1

If the prawns are raw, cook them in boiling water for 5 to 8 minutes and let them cool.

2

Remove the heads, shells and intestinal track (black vein) and reserve.

3

Slice the lettuce into thin shreds.

4

For the dressing, first peel and finely chop the shallots. In a saucepan, on low heat, pickle in white wine until liquid has evaporated then let cool.

5

Pour the mayonnaise in a bowl. Add the mustard, ketchup, Tabasco and Worcestershire sauce.

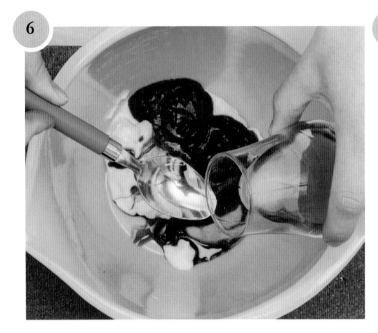

Stir the vinegar and Brandy into the sauce.

Mix all of the sauce ingredients quickly with a whisk.

Stir in melted shallot and chopped tarragon and season to taste with salt and pepper.

Dress the salad in a bowl or glass with the lettuce at the bottom, prawns then Thousand Islands dressing on top.

Dauphinoise Potatoes

Ingredients

8 large potatoes

750 ml / 1 ¼ pt / 3 cups of cream

100 g / 4oz / ⅔ cup of flour

125 g / 4 ½ oz of butter

2 cloves of garlic

2 onions

salt and freshly ground pepper

½ grated nutmeg

60 g / 2 ½ oz / ½ cup grated cheese

SERVES 4 | PREP TIME 15 minutes | COOKING TIME 60 minutes

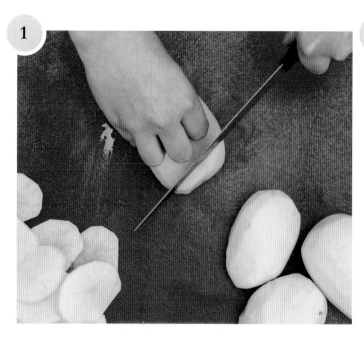

Preheat the oven to 180°C (160° fan) / 350F / gas 4. Peel, rinse and cut the potatoes into thin slices.

Sauté in butter with garlic, onion and salt and pepper.

3

When the onions are golden, remove from the heat, add flour and cream and combine over very low heat. Add the grated nutmeg if you like at that point. If the sauce seems too thick add a little milk.

4

Carefully layer the potato slices in the bottom of the baking dish.

5

Pour the liquid over the top of the potatoes. Repeat until you run out of potatoes and sauce.

6

Bake for 1 hour and add the grated cheese 5 minutes before the end of the cooking with a pinch of black pepper. Serve hot.

Onion Rings

Ingredients

2 large onions

1 egg (white and yolk separated)

200 g / 7 oz / 1 ⅓ cup flour

1 tbsp of milk

½ tbsp of oil

4 tbsp of tomato ketchup (optional)

pinch of salt

SERVES 4 | PREP TIME 10 minutes | COOKING TIME 8 minutes

Peel and slice the onions, separate the slices and set aside.

In a bowl, mix the flour, egg yolk, milk, oil and salt to obtain a smooth paste.

In another bowl, beat the egg white until stiff and fold gently into the previous mixture.

Dip the onions in the batter to coat well.

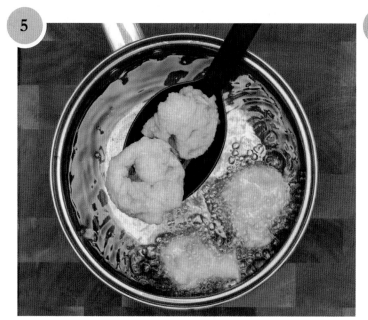

Deep fry in a frying pan filled with hot oil.

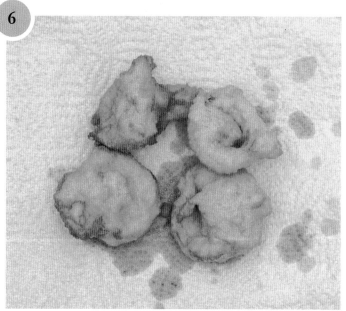

Once they reach a golden colour, remove and place on a sheet of kitchen paper. Serve hot with a ramekin of ketchup, some lemon or dips.

Ratatouille

Ingredients

5 tomatoes

2 aubergines

4 courgettes

3 peppers

2 cloves of garlic

1 onion

2 tbsp olive oil

bouquet garni (thyme, bay leaf)

salt and pepper

SERVES 4 | PREP TIME 20 minutes | COOKING TIME 40 minutes

1

Peel the garlic and onion and cut them into pieces.

2

Wash all the vegetables, cut the aubergines and courgettes, quarter the tomatoes and slice the peppers into strips.

Add the olive oil to a saucepan and heat to a high temperature. Fry the onion and add the vegetables.

Season with salt and pepper, then add the garlic, bay leaf and thyme, bar a couple of sprigs.

Reduce the heat and simmer for 35 minutes, stirring occasionally.

Decorate with thyme sprigs. Ratatouille can be eaten hot or cold.

Cauliflower Cheese

Ingredients

1.2 kg / 2 ½ lb cauliflower

a few chives

20 g / ¾ oz butter

salt

For the sauce:

50 g / 2oz butter

50 g / 2oz / ⅓ cup flour

750 ml / 1 ½ pint / 3 cups milk

70 g / 3oz / ⅔ cup grated cheese

salt and pepper

SERVES 6 | PREP TIME 15 minutes | COOKING TIME 60-70 minutes

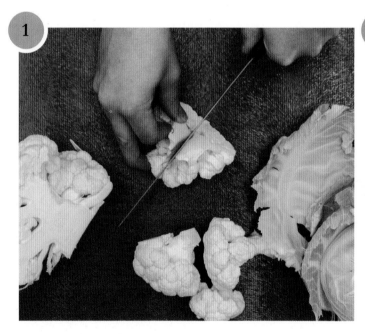

Cut the cauliflower into small florets.

Dip them in boiling salted water and cook for 15 minutes. Drain and keep warm.

Melt the butter in a saucepan. Add the flour and mix to a smooth paste. Pour the milk, salt and pepper and cook, stirring until thickened.

Cook for 10 minutes over a low heat. Remove from the heat, add half the cheese, chives and cauliflower florets. Mix well.

Preheat the oven to 240°C (220° fan) / 475F / gas 9. Pour the mixture of cauliflower into a buttered high edges oven dish.

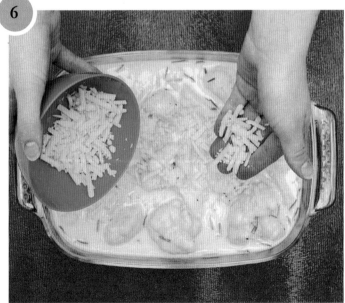

Sprinkle the remaining cheese and dot with butter. Bake for 20 minutes and serve immediately.

Homemade Chips

Ingredients

1 kg / 2 lb 4 oz potatoes

3 cloves of garlic

1 bay leaf

2 l / 3 pints 8 fl. oz / 8 cups vegetable oil

salt

SERVES 6 | PREP TIME 12 minutes | COOKING TIME 30 minutes

Peel the potatoes and cut them into thick chips.

Rinse them and place them in a saucepan in cold water.

Bring the water to the boil then drain the potatoes and rinse them again under cold water.

Peel the garlic and wash the bay leaf. Heat the oil in a deep frying pan.

Fry the chips for 8 minutes, then remove them.

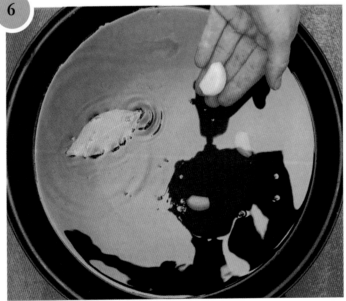

Throw the garlic and bay leaf in the fryer and place the chips back in for 6 to 8 minutes, until golden. Then, remove them, season and serve.

Roast Leg of Lamb

Ingredients

1 kg / 2 lb 4 oz leg of lamb

15 cloves of garlic

50 g / 2 oz / ½ stick of butter

2 bay leaves

2 sprigs fresh thyme

2 tbsp olive oil

sea salt

freshly ground pepper

2 onions

1 broccoli

3 tomatoes

240 ml / 9 fl. oz / 1 cup water

SERVES 6 | PREP TIME 15 minutes | COOKING TIME 50 minutes

Preheat the oven to 200°C (180° fan) / 400F / gas 6 and let the butter soften at room temperature.

Dip the whole and unpeeled garlic cloves in boiling water for 2 minutes then drain.

Put the lamb in a dish and brush it with the softened butter. Sprinkle with olive oil and season with salt and pepper. Sprinkle with bay leaves and thyme.

Pour the water and blanched garlic over the lamb. Place in the oven and bake for 15 minutes per lb, basting regularly with the juice of the leg.

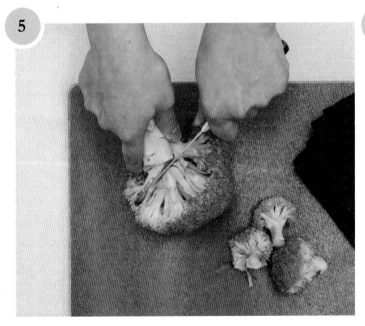

In the meantime, separate the broccoli into florets, and cook in boiling salted until just tender.

Slice the onions and tomatoes and add them to the dish 15 minutes before the end of the cooking. Turn the oven off and leave the lamb to rest for 10 minutes before serving. Add the broccoli to the dish and serve.

Veal Escalope

Ingredients

4 very fine veal escalopes

2 eggs

6 tbsp flour

6 tbsp bread crumbs

3 tbsp grated Parmesan cheese

110 g / 4 oz / 1 stick of butter

chives

salt and pepper

limes for garnish

SERVES 4 | PREP TIME 15 minutes | COOKING TIME 15 minutes

Crack the eggs into a bowl and beat together using a fork. Place the flour in a separate bowl.

Combine the Parmesan cheese and bread crumbs together on a plate.

3

Season the escalopes with salt and pepper.

4

Coat the escalopes with flour and then the then egg mixture.

5

Dip the escalopes in the Parmesan and bread crumbs mix.

6

Fry the escalopes in a little butter in a frying pan for 10 to 12 minutes.
Serve with limes quarters and decorated with a few chopped chives.

Irish Stew

Ingredients

1 kg / 2 lb 4 oz beef sirloin, cubed

500 g / 1 lb 2 oz potatoes, peeled and cut

250 g / 9 oz carrots, sliced

700 g / 1 lb 9 oz onions

3 bay leaves

2 tbsp flour

150 ml / 5 fl. oz / ⅗ cup of stout

1 tsp chopped parsley

2 tbsp oil

salt and pepper

SERVES 4 | PREP TIME 15 minutes | COOKING TIME 90 minutes

Prepare and measure all of the ingredients. Preheat the oven to 140°C (120° fan) / 275F / gas 1.

Heat the oil in a pan and fry the bay leaves. Add the meat, let it brown on all sides, until half cooked.

Add the onions, fry until everything is golden brown.

Sprinkle with flour and combine well.

Pour in the stout, diluted with the same amount of water, ensuring the meat is covered. Season with salt and pepper.

Add the parsley, potatoes and carrots and stir well. Transfer to a casserole dish and place in the oven for 2 hours. Stir halfway through, adding more liquid if necessary. Serve immediately.

Coq au Vin

Ingredients

1 whole rooster (or chicken as an alternative)

40 g / 1 ½ oz / ⅓ stick butter

3 tbsp vegetable oil

250 g / 9 oz of mushrooms

100 g / 4 oz of onions

100 g / 4 oz of carrots

40 g / 1 ½ oz of shallots

40 g / 1 ½ oz of flour

30 g / 1 oz of tomato purée

3 cloves of garlic

750 ml / 1 ½ pints of red wine

60 ml / ¼ cup of cognac / brandy

1 bouquet garni (parsley, thyme, bay leaf)

salt and pepper

SERVES 6 | PREP TIME 15 minutes | COOKING TIME 2 hours

Prepare and measure all of the ingredients.

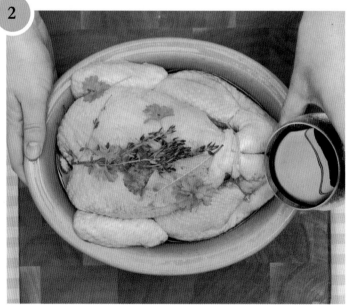

The day before: Place the rooster in a large dish. Sprinkle the bouquet garni over the chicken.

3

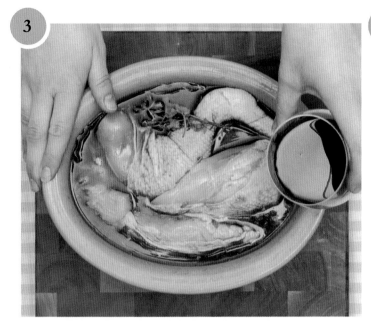

Cover the chicken with red wine and chill in the refrigerator overnight.

4

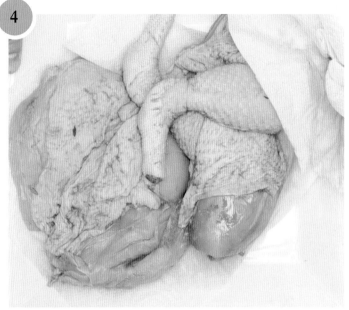

Drain the chicken and pat dry on paper towels. Reserve the marinade.

5

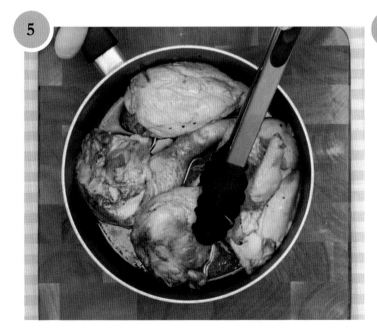

Heat the oil in a pan, add the butter and fry the chicken.
Remove and reserve.

6

Peel and cut the carrots, onions, garlic and shallots.

Add all of the vegetables to a pan and cook gently for 10 minutes.

Sprinkle with flour, stir, add the cognac/brandy and tomato purée.

Then add the chicken, sprinkle with the wine marinade. Season with salt and pepper, simmer gently, and cover for 2 hours.

Wash and slice the mushrooms. Sauté in a pan with oil. Place the chicken in a dish, drizzle with some of the sauce and garnish with the mushrooms. Serve with rice and remaining sauce on the side.

Cannelloni

Ingredients

350 g / 12 oz lasagne sheets

2 cloves of garlic, crushed

1 large onion, finely chopped

1 kg / 2 lb 4 oz finely chopped spinach

2 eggs, beaten

650 g / 1 lb 10 ½ oz fresh ricotta beaten

pinch of freshly grated nutmeg

2 tbsp olive oil

For the tomato sauce:

1 medium onion, chopped

450 g / 1 lb ripe tomatoes, chopped

2 cloves of garlic, finely chopped

2 tbsp tomato paste

150 g / 5 oz mozzarella, cut into small pieces

1 tsp brown sugar

1 tbsp olive oil

SERVES 6 | PREP TIME 40 minutes | COOKING TIME 75 minutes

Prepare and measure all of the ingredients.

Bring a saucepan of water to the boil and immerse 2 lasagna sheets at a time until they soften.

3

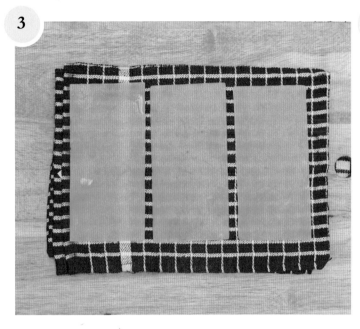

Carefully remove each sheet with a slotted spoon and lay them flat on a clean cloth.

4

Heat the oil in a frying pan and brown the onion and garlic over low heat for 10 minutes, stirring occasionally. Add the washed spinach and cook for 2 minutes before covering the pan tightly. Simmer for 5 minutes then drain as much juice as possible.

5

In a bowl, mix the spinach, ricotta, eggs, nutmeg, salt and pepper.

6

Heat the oil in a pan and fry the garlic and onion over a low heat for 5 minutes. Add the chopped tomatoes and their juice, tomato paste, sugar, 150 ml / 5 fl. oz of water, salt and pepper. Bring to the boil and then simmer for 10 minutes.

7

Preheat the oven to 180°C (160° fan) / 350F / gas 4 and lightly butter a baking dish. Spread ⅓ of the tomato sauce at the bottom. Place 2 tbsp of mix in the centre of each lasagna sheet, then roll the dough around the filling and place in the dish, seam down.

8

Repeat with the remaining lasagna sheets, then pour the remaining tomato sauce over the cannelloni and sprinkle with mozzarella. Bake for 35 minutes, until the cannelloni are golden and the sauce is bubbly. Let it cool for 10 minutes before serving.

Beef Bourgignon

Ingredients

1.3 kg / 3 lb of stewing beef

150 g / 5 oz of smoked bacon

2 carrots

1 large onion

200 g / 7 oz of small white onions

½ bottle red wine

1 clove garlic

1 cube beef stock

3 sprigs parsley

2 tbsp cooking oil

salt and pepper

SERVES 4 | PREP TIME 30 minutes | COOKING TIME 3 hours

Carefully prepare the meat and cut into cubes. Peel and chop the garlic and the large onion. Chop the bacon into lardoons. Peel the carrots, wash them, cut them into medium sized slices.

Heat the oil in a casserole. Cook the bacon for 5 minutes, then add the onions, carrots and garlic.

Fry for another 5 minutes, then drain using a slotted spoon. Place the meat cubes in the pan and let them brown on all sides.

Add the bacon and vegetables to the meat (except small onions).

Pour in the wine and beef stock in the casserole. Add salt and pepper, parsley, cover and cook for 2 hours 30 minutes over medium heat.

About 15 minutes before the end of cooking, add the small onions to the casserole. Serve piping hot.

Shepherd's Pie

Ingredients

600 g / 1 lb 5 oz lamb mince

100 g / 4 oz ham

5 shallots

1 bouquet garni

1 bunch parsley

200 ml / 7 oz / ⅝ cup beef stock

1.3 kg / 3 lb potatoes

40 ml milk

110 g / 4 oz / 1 cup grated cheese

110 g / 4 oz / 1 stick of butter

salt and pepper

SERVES 6 | PREP TIME 15 minutes | COOKING TIME 40 minutes

Preheat the oven to 210°C (190° fan) / 420F / gas 7. Chop the ham, shallots and parsley.

Cook the lamb mince in a frying pan with one third of the butter.

Mix the meat in a bowl with the ham, shallots and parsley. Add salt and pepper, cover with beef stock and mix well.

Boil the potatoes in a pan with cold water, until tender. Add ⅓ of the butter and milk to the potatoes and mash them thoroughly.

Butter a baking dish and spread the meat at the bottom. Top with the mashed potatoes.

Sprinkle with cheese and bake in the oven for 30 minutes. Serve with seasonal vegetables.

Spaghetti Bolognaise

Ingredients

250 g / 9 oz spaghetti pasta

150 g / 5 oz ground veal or pork

150 g / 5 oz ground beef

60 g / 2 ½ oz / ½ cup grated Parmesan
cheese

2 tbsp olive oil

salt and pepper

For the sauce:

1 can of chopped tomatoes

2 shallots

3 basil leaves

6 sprigs of rosemary

olive oil

salt and pepper

SERVES 4 | PREP TIME 10 minutes | COOKING TIME 25 minutes

Drain the chopped tomatoes in a colander. Peel and chop the shallots and fry with oil, adding the tomatoes, basil and rosemary sprigs.

Season with salt and pepper and simmer 15 minutes. In a frying pan, cook the ground veal/pork with olive oil over a very low heat for 10 minutes.

Add the beef and cook for 5 minutes, stirring occasionally.

Then add the tomato sauce, salt and pepper and cook for another 10 minutes.

Meanwhile, boil a large quantity of salted water in a saucepan; add 1 tbsp of olive oil and the spaghetti. Cook for 10 minutes, the pasta should remain "al dente". Drain.

Mix the pasta and sauce together in a bow. Serve piping hot, sprinkled with Parmesan.

Four Season Pizza

Ingredients

For the pizza dough:

300 g / 11 oz / 2 cups wheat flour

120 ml / 4 fl. oz / ½ cup warm water

20 g / ¾ oz of yeast

½ tsp salt

2 tbsp olive oil

For the filling:

2 peppers

125 g / 4 ½ oz mushrooms

2 tomatoes

50 g / 2 oz / ⅓ cup black olives

4 tbsp tomato sauce

1 clove of garlic

60 g / 2 ½ oz / ½ cup of grated mozzarella

parsley to sprinkle

olive oil

salt and pepper

SERVES 6 | PREP TIME 30 minutes | COOKING TIME 15 minutes

Put the flour in a bowl, form a hole in the centre and crumble in the yeast then add the salt. Combine with warm water and form a ball.

Let rest 15 minutes in a warm place. Add olive oil and work the dough again. Form a ball again and cover it with flour. Wrap in a towel and let rest for 15 minutes.

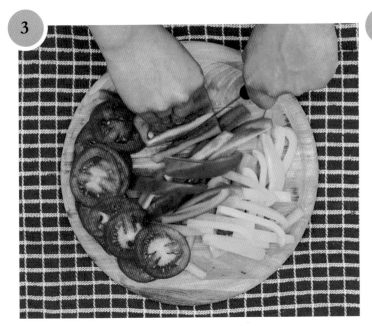

Preheat the oven at 200°C (180° fan) / 400F / gas 6. Slice the peppers into thin strips and the tomatoes then set aside.

Heat a little olive oil in a frying pan and add the mushrooms. Sauté a few minutes with garlic, parsley, a pinch of salt. Reserve them.

Roll out the pizza dough to obtain a 30 cm / 12" in circle. Spread the tomato sauce on the pizza dough.

Cover with the mushrooms, the peppers and the tomatoes. Sprinkle with a few sliced black olives, the mozzarella cheese, a turn of pepper and a drizzle of olive oil and bake in the oven for about 15 minutes.

Chicken and Mushroom Pie

Ingredients

2 shortcrust pastry packs

4 chicken breasts

5 slices of smoked ham

2 leeks

1 onion or 2 shallots

200 g / 7 oz of button mushroom

1 egg and 1 yolk

125 ml / 4 ½ fl. oz / ½ cup of white wine

350 ml / 12 fl. oz / 1 ½ cup of cream

50 g / 2 oz / ½ cup of grated cheese

pinch of paprika

salt and pepper

SERVES 4 | PREP TIME 15 minutes | COOKING TIME 45 minutes

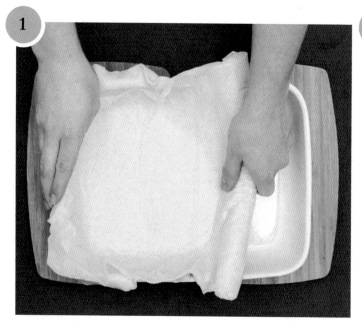

Preheat the oven to 180°C (160° fan) / 350F / gas 4. Roll out the puff pastry into a pie dish.

Blind bake for 10 minutes, covered with foil and weighted down with rice or beans.

Cut the leeks into thin slices, chop the onions and mushrooms and cut the chicken breasts into small pieces. Saute the onions in a pan with some butter; add the leeks and mushrooms and let cook for 10 minutes covered.

Add salt and pepper, add the paprika and deglaze with white wine, stir everything together and drop it onto the dough already spread and add the cheese.

Meanwhile fry the chopped chicken and smoked ham in a pan, and scatter it also on the pastry.

6

Beat the egg and add the cream. Mix and pour over the ingredients.

7

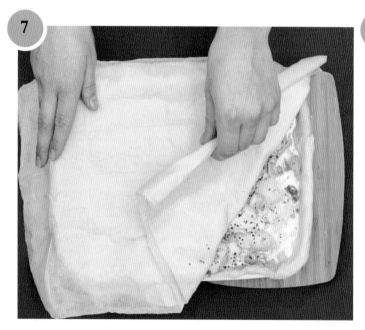

Add the cheese and cover with the second crust.

8

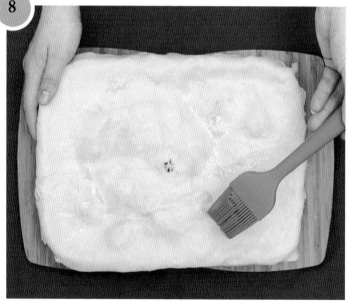

Make a hole at the centre of the pastry top, and decorate the pastry with a knife. Beat the egg yolk and with a brush put a little yellow on the top of the pie so that it has a nice golden colour. Bake for 30 to 45 minutes. Serve hot with a seasonal salad.

Seafood Paella

Ingredients

12 prawns

18 mussels

450 g / 1 lb of cockles

450 g / 1 lb of squid

2 lobsters

6 tomatoes

200 g / 7 oz garden peas

600 g / 1 lb 5 oz / 3 cups long grain rice

1 bunch of parsley

1 tsp powdered saffron

1.5 l / 3 pints fish stock

2 cloves of garlic

7 tbsp olive oil

salt and pepper

1 lemon

SERVES 6 | PREP TIME 35 minutes | COOKING TIME 30 minutes

Blanch the tomatoes. Remove from the heat, then peel and blend them.

In a saucepan, boil the mussels and cockerels, until the shells open. Remove from the heat but leave the shells on.

3

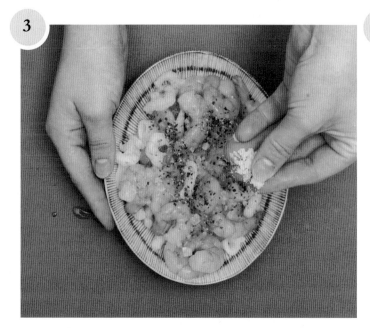

4

Peel and chop the garlic. Wash and chop the parsley. Shell the prawns leaving only the tails. Cut the squid into strips. Season everything and keep refrigerated.

Cook the lobster in boiling water after placing in the freezer for 10 minutes. Shell the lobsters, and reserve the claws. You can substitute with crab or crayfish. Sauté the squid in 4 tbsp of olive oil. Simmer for 5 minutes.

5

Add the garlic and parsley to the tomatoes. Place the prawn tails in the remaining olive oil. Stir in the tomato sauce and a pinch of saffron. Mix well.

6

7

Combine the rice, two-thirds of the stock and the saffron in a wok or large pan. Stir and boil for 10 minutes.

In the meantime boil the peas in salted boiling water till tender.

8

Halfway through cooking the rice, add the remaining fish stock. Serve the rice on a serving dish and garnish with the seafood. Accompany with lemon wedges.

Roast Chicken Breast

Ingredients

3 chicken breasts

2 lemons

10 cloves of garlic

8 sage leaves

1 sprig of thyme

3 sprigs of rosemary

1 cinnamon stick

50 ml / 2 fl. oz / ⅕ cup dry white wine

1 tbsp of flour

2 tbsp of olive oil

salt and pepper

SERVES 4 | PREP TIME 20 minutes | COOKING TIME 60 minutes

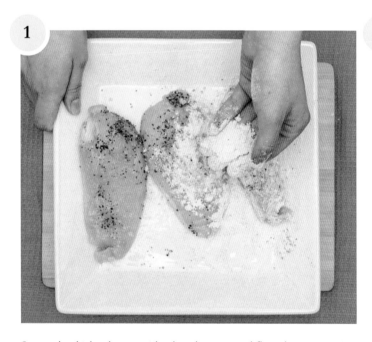

Season the chicken breasts with salt and pepper, and flour them.

Blanch the garlic, unpeeled, in boiling water for a few minutes. Chop the thyme and rosemary finely.

3

Heat the oil in a frying pan. Brown the chicken breast for 10 minutes, turning.

4

Remove and place in a baking dish then sprinkle with the dry white wine and herbs.

5

Add the garlic cloves and cinnamon stick.

6

Cut the lemon centres into 1cm / ½ inch slices, extract the juice from the rest and reserve. Place in the oven for 40 minutes. Halfway through, turn them and add the slices of lemon and sage leaves.

Wellington Steak

Ingredients

750 g / 1 lb 10 ½ oz of beef fillet

pinch of paprika

2 sprigs of thyme

pinch of curry powder

1 tbsp cooking oil

¾ tbsp. salt

pepper

For the mushroom duxelle:

200 g / 7 oz of button mushrooms

100 g / 4 oz of pork sausage

1 tbsp lemon juice

1 tsp herbs (thyme/rosemary)

1 tbsp butter

½ tsp salt

For the crust:

450 g / 1 lb puff pastry

1 egg

SERVES 4 | PREP TIME 20 minutes | COOKING TIME 40 minutes

Preheat the oven to 200°C (180° fan) / 400F / gas 6. Rub the beef with paprika, curry powder and thyme.

Heat the oil and sear the meat quickly on all sides. Let it cool and reserve the fillet.

To prepare the duxelle, clean the mushrooms and chop finely. Heat the butter in a pan, add the sausage meat, salt, mushrooms, mixed herbs and lemon juice. Sauté over a high heat so that the liquid evaporates and reserve.

To prepare the crust, roll the pastry into a rectangle, 2 mm thick. Cut a rectangle large enough to wrap around the fillet. Place the meat in the middle and coat it with the duxelle.

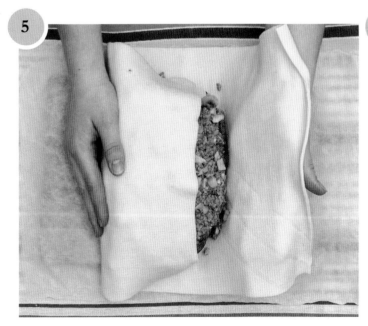

Fold the dough and then seal the edges with egg white. Place on an oiled baking sheet and sealed edge underneath.

Score the surface of the dough with patterns, brush with egg yolk and prick with a fork. Bake for 40 minutes. Let it stand for a few minutes before serving. Serve with asparagus.

Stuffed Chicken Breast

Ingredients

2 chicken breasts (not too thick, skin on)

1 ball of mozzarella

3 sun-dried tomatoes

20 fresh basil leaves

5 small ripe tomatoes

1 onion, chopped

240 ml / 9 fl. oz / 1 cup of dry white wine

olive oil

salt and pepper

SERVES 2 | PREP TIME 15 minutes | COOKING TIME 45 minutes

Butterfly the chicken breasts using a sharp knife.

Slice 3 tomatoes and the sun-dried tomatoes. Slice the mozzarella ball into thin slices.

Mix together 15 basil leaves, all of the sliced mozzarella, sliced fresh tomatoes and sliced sun-dried tomatoes.

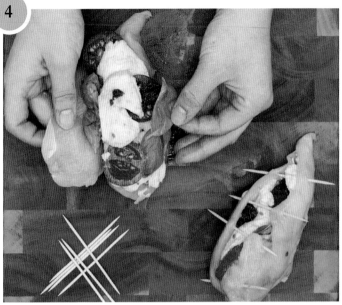

Place half of the mixture on each flattened breast. Then close up the chicken breast slice and secure using toothpicks, in order to keep everything tight.

Peel, seed and cut the 2 remaining fresh tomatoes. Chop and sauté the onion in olive oil.

Pour the tomatoes, onions and white wine into a baking dish and season with salt and pepper. Place the breasts on top. Bake for 45 minutes at 200°C (180° fan) / 400F / gas 6, adding small quantities of water to stop the breasts becoming dry.

Vegetable Lasagna

Ingredients

12 lasagna sheets

6 medium courgettes

2 medium aubergines

4 tomatoes

1 yellow pepper

450 g / 1lb fresh spinach

3 tbsp crème fraiche

60 g / 2 ½ oz / ½ cup of mozzarella

2 tbsp chopped basil

6 tbsp olive oil

salt and pepper

SERVES 6 | PREP TIME 30 minutes | COOKING TIME 45 minutes

Preapare and measure all of the ingredients. Wash the basil leaves.

Cut the courgettes, aubergines, yellow pepper and tomatoes into slices.

3

Heat 3 tbsp of oil in a pan and fry the aubergines. Add the courgette and cook for 5 minutes, stirring. Add the tomatoes, pepper and basil, reduce the heat and season with salt and pepper.

4

Cover and cook for 30 minutes, stirring occasionally.

5

Cook the lasagna sheets in boiling salted water for the time indicated on the package.

6

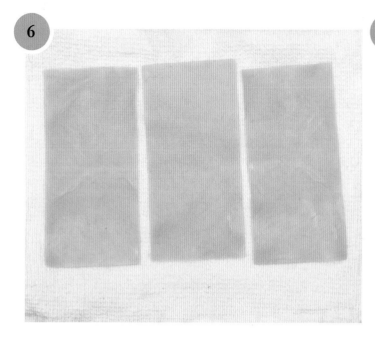

Drain them and place them on a cloth. Wash the spinach.

7

Heat the remaining oil in a frying pan and fry the spinach gently for 15 min. Season with salt and pepper, add the crème fraiche and mix well. Preheat the oven to 170°C (150° fan) / 325F / gas 3.

8

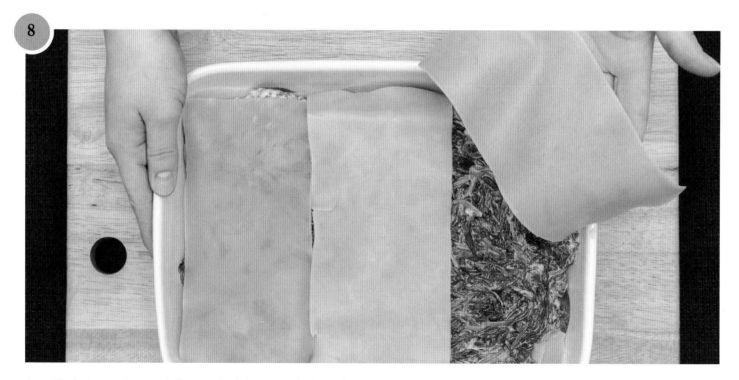

Assemble the lasagna sheets at the bottom of a dish, cover with a layer of the vegetables, then spinach and keep layering until you run out of vegetables. The last layer should be lasagna sheets. Sprinkle with mozzarella and bake for 20 minutes.

Roast Chicken

Ingredients

1.5 kg / 3 lb 5 oz fresh chicken

1 tbsp mustard

1 tbsp mixed herbs

2 cubes chicken stock

1 bay leaf

600 g / 1 lb 5 oz white potatoes

400 g / 14 oz sweet potatoes

400 g / 14 oz carrots

1 tbsp butter

salt and pepper

SERVES 4 | PREP TIME 15 minutes | COOKING TIME 40 minutes

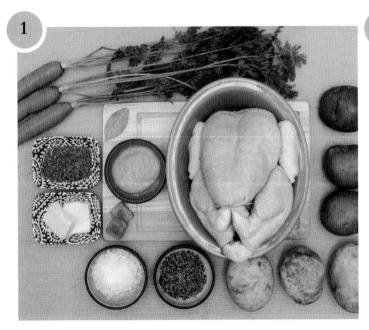

Prepare and measure all of the ingredients. Preheat the oven to 200°C (180° fan) / 400F / gas 6.

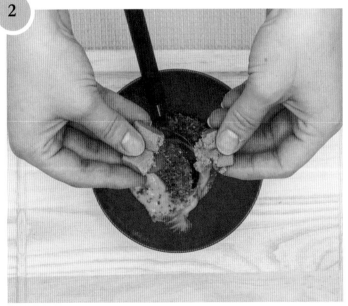

Mix together the mustard, herbs and 1 crumbled cube of stock.

3

Brush the inside and the outside of the chicken with the mustard mix.

4

Mix the other cube of chicken stock, the bay leaf and two large glasses of water in a bowl. Place the chicken in a colander, above the broth.

5

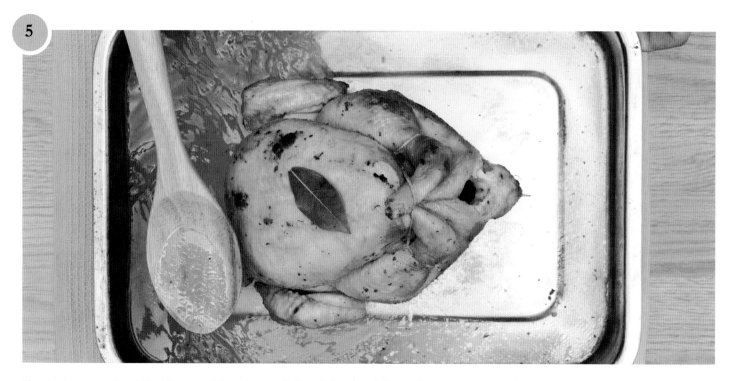

Place in the oven and cook for 25 minutes. Then place in a baking dish and cook for another 20 minutes while basting with the juice every 5 minutes.

6

Peel and cut the carrots into batons. Cook the batons in boiling water until still.

7

Place the carrots with the chicken for the last 15 minutes in the oven to roast.

8

Peel the white and sweet potatoes and cut them into chips. Fry them in hot oil until thoroughly cooked. Place the chips in the chicken dish and sprinkle with salt.

Chicken Curry

Ingredients

750 g / 1 lb 10 ½ oz chicken

2 onions, finely chopped

2 cloves garlic

1 chopped red chilli

oil

150 g / 5 oz natural yoghurt

150 ml / 5 fl. oz / ⅝ cup cream

50 g / 2 oz of cashew nuts

2 roots minced fresh ginger

1 cinnamon stick

cardamom powder

6 cloves

2 teaspoons chopped fresh cilantro

1 tablespoon coriander seeds

saffron or turmeric powder

salt and pepper

SERVES 4 | PREP TIME 40 minutes | COOKING TIME 45 minutes

Grind the ginger, garlic, chilli, coriander seeds, half of the cashew nuts and 1 onion in a mortar, then add the mix to a glass of water in a bowl and salt.

Brush the chicken pieces with this mixture and marinate in the refrigerator for at least 1 hour.

Chop the second onion, fry it in oil with a little powdered cardamom, cloves and cinnamon, until the onions are transparent.

Add the chicken with marinade, simmer until the juice has almost completely evaporated.

Add the yogurt, cover and simmer 30 minutes over very low heat.

Add the remaining cashew nuts, fresh cream and saffron, pour over chicken, check seasoning and simmer for another 5 min. Serve with rice, flat bread or poppadoms.

Beef and Carrot Stew

Ingredients

1 kg / 2 lb 4oz of stewing beef

1 kg / 2 lb 4oz of carrots

2 onions

5 shallots

1 tablespoon of flour

300 ml / 11 fl. oz / 1 ¼ cup of white wine

250 ml / 9 fl. oz / 1 cup of water

2 tbsp olive oil

1 bouquet garni (thyme, bay leak, parsley)

salt and pepper

SERVES 6 | PREP TIME 25 minutes | COOKING TIME 2 hours

Cut the meat into pieces. Peel and slice the onions.

In a casserole dish heat the oil, then add the chopped onions and let them brown with the meat.

3

Sprinkle with a tablespoon of flour and mix well.

4

Pour in the white wine, water, and add the bouquet garni. Season with salt and pepper, then cover and simmer for 1 hour.

5

Peel the carrots and shallots. Slice the carrots and add them and the shallots to the casserole. Cook for 1 hour. Serve hot or reheat for the next day.

Macaroni Cheese

Ingredients

250 g / 9 oz macaroni pasta
4 slices of ham
125 g / 4 ½ oz / 1 ⅔ cups button
mushrooms
60 g / 2 ½ oz / ½ cup grated cheese
1 tbsp olive oil
salt and pepper

For the bechamel:
40 g / 1 ½ oz / ⅓ stick of butter
40 g / 1 ½ oz plain flour
600 ml / 1 pt 2 fl. oz milk
salt and pepper

SERVES 4 | PREP TIME 20 minutes | COOKING TIME 20 minutes

Cook the macaroni, according to the instructions on the package.

Meanwhile, prepare the béchamel by melting the butter in a saucepan over
a medium heat. Add the flour and stir for a few minutes to cook a roux,
then add the milk gradually and cook for 15 minutes until the sauce is thick
and smooth.

Cut the ham into small pieces and brown it for a few minutes with the mushrooms in a non-stick pan with the olive oil.

Pour the macaroni, ham and mushrooms into an ovenproof baking dish.

Add the white sauce and season with salt and pepper.

Top the dish with cheese and bake for 10 minutes in the grill oven to brown the cheese slightly.

Chilli con Carne

Ingredients

600 g / 1 lb 5 oz ground beef

300 g / 11 oz / 1 ½ cup dry kidney beans

2 large tomatoes

2 cloves garlic

2 large onions

250 ml / 8 fl. oz / 1 cup tomato sauce

2 teaspoons of cumin

1 tablespoon dried oregano

½ teaspoon chilli powder

olive oil

400 g / 13 oz / 2 cups of rice

salt and pepper

SERVES 4 | PREP TIME 45 minutes | COOKING TIME 2 hours

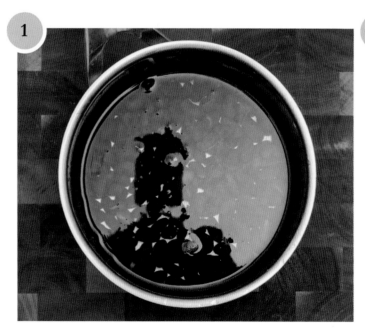

Soak the beans for 12 hours in cold water, then cook in fresh water for 1 ½ hours on low heat and season with salt.

Chop the onions and garlic and fry them in a pan with oil until translucent. Add the ground meat, mix and stir over medium heat.

3

Add the tomatoes peeled, seeded and diced, the chilli powder, oregano and cumin.

4

Add the tomato sauce and leave to simmer for 5 minutes.

5

Drain the beans and add to mixture. Stir and cook for 20 minutes over low heat.

6

Meanwhile cook the rice in boiling salted water, drain and reserve. Adjust the seasoning of the sauce to taste and serve over the rice.

Mussels in White Wine

Ingredients

4 kg / 9 lbs whole mussels

4 onions

5 cloves of garlic

250 ml / 9 fl. oz / 1 cup dry white wine

splash of cream

110 g / 4 oz / 1 stick of butter

SERVES 6 | PREP TIME 15 minutes | COOKING TIME 20 minutes

Prepare and measure all of the ingredients. Place the mussels in a bowl.

Clean the mussels by washing them thoroughly in cold running water.
Discard all the opened mussels.

Cook the mussels on a medium heat with the butter, onions and garlic.

Add the white wine and gently simmer until the mussels open.

When the mussels are cooked, add the cream and stir well.

Sprinkle with fresh chopped parsley. Serve with crispy chips and a glass of dry white wine.

Moussaka

Ingredients

400 g / 14 oz ground minced beef

3 medium aubergines

2 medium onions

4 large tomatoes

3 eggs

50 g / 2 oz / ½ stick of butter

750 ml / 1 pint 6 fl. oz / 3 cups milk

250 ml / 9 fl. oz / 1 cup dry white wine

250 ml / 9 fl. oz / 1 cup olive oil

100 g / 4 oz / 1 cup breadcrumbs

100 g / 4 oz / 1 cup grated Parmesan

2 tsp lemon juice

4 tbsp flour

¼ tsp sugar

½ tsp cinnamon

1 tsp dried oregano

bunch of parsley

1 freshly grated nutmeg

salt and pepper

SERVES 4 | PREP TIME 5 hours 30 minutes | COOKING TIME 1 hour

Wash the aubergines and cut them into 1 cm slices. Plunge them in cold water for 20 minutes then drain in a sieve and dry with paper towels.

Heat 3 or 4 tbsp of oil in a non-stick pan and brown the aubergine slices in batches, on both sides then remove them with a wooden spatula and place them on absorbent paper.

Peel the onions and chop them. Peel the tomatoes and cut them into pieces. Cook the onions in the oil from the aubergines, then add the ground meat and cook it on a high heat, until the juices have evaporated.

Stir in the tomatoes, wine and sprinkle with salt, sugar, cinnamon and pepper then cook, covered, for 5 minutes, over moderate heat.

Wash and chop the parsley and oregano, mix them with the mince and cook for 5 minutes. Remove from the heat and add the breadcrumbs and half of the cheese. Preheat the oven to 170°C (150° fan) / 325F / gas 3.

Melt the butter in a saucepan and add the flour. Whisk well before adding the milk in a slow, steady stream whisking simultaneously. Simmer for 5 minutes over a low heat, stirring occasionally

7

Season with salt, pepper, nutmeg and lemon juice, stirring continuously.

8

Beat 2 eggs using a whisk and add them to the sauce.

9

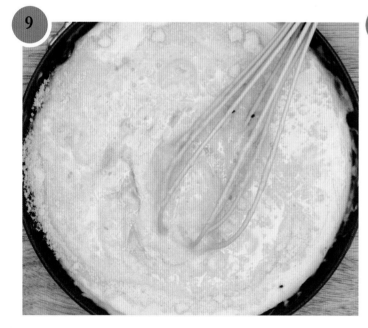

Add the remaining cheese and stir well, ensuring the cheese completely melts. Coat a baking dish with butter and add half of the aubergines.

10

Beat the egg and add it to the mince. Spread it over the aubergines. Reserve 2 tbsp of minced meat. Add another layer of aubergines, the mince and top with cheese sauce. Cook in the oven for 1 hour.

Spaghetti Carbonara

Ingredients

450 g / 1 lb spaghetti

50 g / 2 oz bacon

50 g / 2 oz / ½ cup pecorino cheese, grated

2 eggs

2 cloves of garlic

1 tbsp oil

1 tbsp extra virgin olive oil

4 tbsp double cream

salt and white pepper

½ tsp finely chopped parsley

SERVES 4 | PREP TIME 10 minutes | COOKING TIME 20 minutes

Prepare and measure all of the ingredients. Grate the cheese.

Fill a saucepan with water and bring to the boil. Add 1 ½ tsp of salt and 1 tbsp of oil. Add the spaghetti, stirring gently with a fork and cook al dente, for about 8 minutes.

Drain the spaghetti using a colander and reserve.

Cut the bacon into thin strips. Peel the garlic cloves and cut them into quarters in length.

Sauté the garlic in olive oil then remove the garlic from the pan to replace it with the bacon that you let brown for a few minutes.

Break the eggs into a dish and beat them with cream.

Add the cheese and season with salt and pepper.

Add the spaghetti to the bacon in the frying pan over a low heat. Let them warm up for a few minutes.

Pour the pasta and bacon in a serving dish. Mix everything then sprinkle the chopped parsley on top. Serve immediately.

Quiche Lorraine

Ingredients

1 packet of short cut pastry

250 g / 9 oz / 1 ⅔ cups plain (all-purpose)
flour

1 egg

pinch of salt

125 g / 4 ½ oz / 1 cup softened butter

For the filling:

3 eggs

150 ml / 5 fl. oz / ⅔ cup cream

150 g / 5 oz bacon

200 g / 7 oz / 2 cups of cheese

SERVES 4 | PREP TIME 10 minutes | COOKING TIME 40 minutes

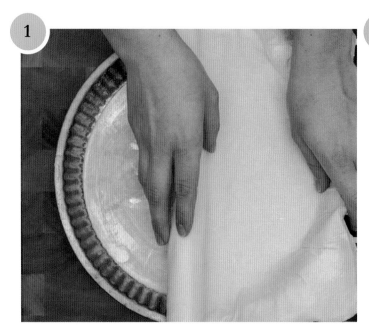

Preheat the oven to 200°C (180° fan) / 400F / gas 6. Spread the dough and place it in a pie dish that has been buttered and floured, leaving it beyond the edges.

Cut the bacon and cheese into small cubes.

3

Break the eggs into a bowl and beat them well.

4

Add the bacon, cheese and cream. Season with a pinch of pepper.

5

Mix well before pouring over the pastry, into the pie dish.

6

Slowly fold the overflowing pastry over the filling. Bake for 40 minutes. Prick with a sharp knife to see if it is well cooked through. Serve with green salad.

Cottage Pie

Ingredients

600 g / 1 lb 5 oz ground beef

1 kg / 2 lb 4oz potatoes

30 ml / 1 fl. oz / ⅛ cup milk

2 onions

1 carrot

80 g / 3 oz / ⅔ stick butter

pinch of ground nutmeg

4 sprigs of parsley

1 l / 1 pint 16 fl. oz / 4 cups beef stock

salt and pepper

SERVES 4 | PREP TIME 30 minutes | COOKING TIME 80 minutes

Preapare and measure all of the ingredients. Peel, wash and cut the potatoes into large cubes.

Cook the potatoes in cold water brought to the boil, until tender in the centre.

3

In a pan melt a third of the butter. Finely chop the onions and sauté for 5 minutes. Add the meat to the pan. Cut the carrot into small cubes and add to the meat.

4

Season with salt and pepper. Mix well and cook for 15 minutes over a medium heat while stirring occasionally.

5

Preheat the oven to 210°C (190° fan) / 425F / gas 7. Drain the potatoes and mash them while still warm. Mix with hot milk and another third of the butter. Season with salt and pepper. Add the ground nutmeg.

6

Place the meat in a baking dish greased with the remaining butter and the mashed potatoes on top, and bake in the oven for 30 minutes. Decorate with parsley and serve with vegetables.

Chicken Tikka

Ingredients

6 chicken breasts

2 natural yoghurts

1 onion

3 cloves garlic

5 cm / 2 inches fresh ginger

1 tsp turmeric, 1 tsp of cumin powder

1 tsp garam masala

1 pinch chilli powder

1 teaspoon cooking oil

salt and pepper

400 g / 14 oz / 2 cups basmati rice

2 tbsp butter

½ tsp saffron threads

450 ml / 16 fl. oz / 1 ⅘ cups vegetable stock

SERVES 6 | PREP TIME 15 minutes | COOKING TIME 10 minutes

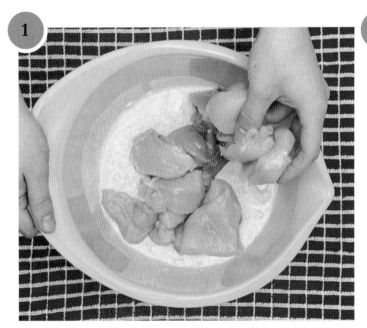

Cut the chicken into cubes and place into a bowl.

In a baking dish, mix the yogurt with finely chopped onion, garlic, grated ginger, spices and oil, then lightly salt and pepper.

Add the marinade to the bowl of chicken and coat it well. Place in the fridge for 3 hours. Rinse the rice under cold water, melting the butter in a frying pan then add the rinsed rice and cook for a couple of minutes.

Meanwhile, soak the saffron for a couple of minutes in 1 tbsp of hot water.

Add it to the rice with hot vegetable stock and 450 ml / a pint of water, boil and then simmer for 15 minutes.

Preheat the oven to 230°C (210° fan) / 450F / gas 8. Cook the chicken for 10 minutes, turning the the pieces regularly. Serve right out of the oven with the basmati rice.

Beef Casserole

Ingredients

1 kg / 2 lb 4 oz beef chuck

100 g / 4 oz of bacon

700 g / 1 lb 9 oz of carrot

250 g / 9 oz of Portobello mushrooms

2 courgettes

1 large onion

1 bunch of parsley

250 ml / 9 fl. oz / 1 cup dry white wine

2 tbsp oil

1 sprig of thyme, 1 bay leaf

2 cloves of garlic

salt and pepper

SERVES 4 | PREP TIME 20 minutes | COOKING TIME 140 minutes

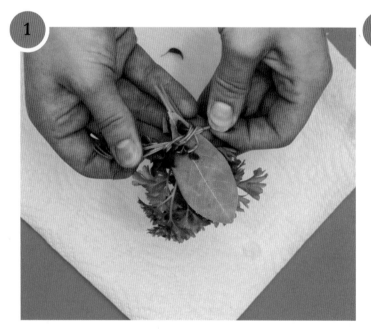

Wash the parsley, pat dry, then make a bouquet garni (parsley tied with the bay leaf and thyme). Cut the meat into large cubes.

Peel and chop the onion, and slice the bacon. In a saucepan, heat oil over moderate heat, fry the onion and bacon, remove and set to one side.

Add the meat to the saucepan and brown on all sides.

Place the bacon and onions in the saucepan, add salt and pepper and pour the white wine, add 250 ml of water, bouquet garni and 2 crushed garlic cloves.

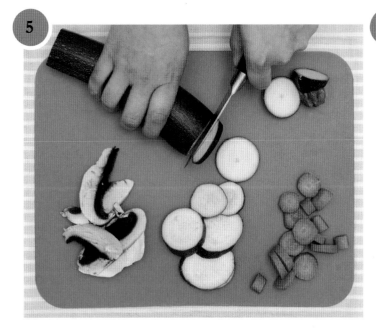

Cover, reduce the heat to the maximum and let braise for 1 hour 30 minutes. Peel, wash and slice the carrots and courgettes. Wash and slice the mushrooms, also.

Check the seasoning of the meat, adding a little water if necessary and add all of the vegetables. Continue cooking, covered, for 45 minutes over low heat. Serve hot, and this dish is even better the next day!

Beef Hamburger

Ingredients

600 g / 1 lb 5 oz minced beef

60 g / 2 ½ oz / ½ cup grated Parmesan

2 tbsp balsamic vinegar

4 tbsp water

bunch of basil leaves

4 buns

4 lettuce leaves

1 onion

1 tomato

tomato ketchup

mayonnaise

olive oil

salt and pepper

4 slices of cheese (optional, for cheeseburger)

SERVES 4 | PREP TIME 20 minutes | COOKING TIME 15 minutes

Preheat the oven to 220°C (200° fan) / 425F / gas 7. Prepare and measure all of the ingredients.

Cut the onions into rings, reserve some for decoration and brown the rest in a frying pan with a drizzle of olive oil. Remove from the heat and reserve.

3

Warm the bread in the oven for 10 minutes. To prepare the burgers, mix the minced beef, Parmesan cheese and finely chopped basil.

4

Mix well using your hands until you obtain a homogeneous stuffing texture. Season with salt and pepper to taste.

5

Using your hands, form four balls fromt he mixture, then flatten to form four burgers.

6

Cook the burgers in the pan used for the onions, for 4 or 5 minutes; season with salt and pepper.

7

On each bread roll, spread a dollop of mayonnaise and ketchup. Place a lettuce leaf on the bottom half of the buns and top with some of the cooked onions.

8

When the burgers are cooked, place a slice of cheese on each (if you like) then place the burgers on the bottom half of the bun and place in the oven for 2 minutes. Place a slice of tomato and some onion rings on top of the burgers. Serve with French Fries.

Traditional Lasagna

Ingredients

For the meat :

400 g / 14 oz ground minced beef

500 ml / 18 fl. oz / 2 cups tomato sauce

20 g / ¾ oz butter

1 large onion

2 medium carrots

1 clove garlic

1 tsp chopped fresh basil

3 pinches of grated nutmeg

4 tbsp olive oil

salt and pepper

For the bechamel sauce:

1 l / 1 pint 16 fl. oz / 4 cups milk

75 g / 3 oz / ½ cup flour

75 g / 3 oz / ⅔ stick butter

salt

pinchs of grated nutmeg

For the lasagna:

9 lasagna sheets

250 g / 9 oz / 2 ½ cups grated Parmesan

SERVES 6 | PREP TIME 30 minutes | COOKING TIME 90 minutes

1

Peel, wash and slice the onions, carrots and garlic. In a saucepan over a medium heat, fry 3 tbsp of olive oil and the butter. Throw in the vegetables. Cover and reduce the heat. Cook for 15 minutes, stirring occasionally.

2

In a large frying pan over high heat, sauté the minced beef in a tablespoon of olive oil for about 5 minutes. The meat should be cooked through. Season.

3

Pour the minced beef into the pan, mix well with a wooden spoon, then pour in the tomato sauce, nutmeg, basil, and season with salt and pepper. Mix well, reduce the heat, cover and simmer for 30 minutes, stirring occasionally.

4

Melt the butter in a large saucepan then whisk in the flour to form a roux. Whisk until smooth, cooking it over a low heat for 1 minute, making sure it does not brown.

5

Add the milk all at once and stir vigorously with a whisk to avoid lumps then increase the heat until the sauce comes to a boil before reducing to a simmer, whisking constantly until it thickens.

6

Season with grated nutmeg and salt. Preheat the oven to 180°C (160° fan) / 350F / gas 4. Grease a large baking dish. Pour a thin layer of béchamel sauce in the dish.

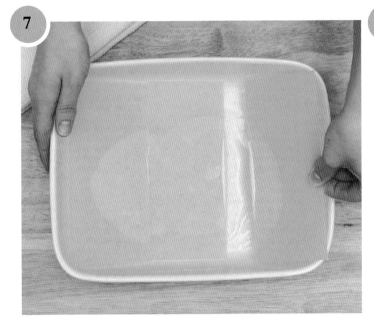

Cover the béchamel sauce with 3 lasagne sheets.

Pour some more béchamel sauce and sprinkle with grated Parmesan cheese.

Place 3 lasagna sheets as the first time, then pour a layer of meat sauce and sprinkle with Parmesan cheese.

Add the last 3 lasagna sheets, then the remaining béchamel sauce and meat sauce and finish with Parmesan. Bake for 35 minutes and serve immediately with grated Parmesan.

Roast Pork with Apples

Ingredients

1 pork fillet (about 800 g / 1 lb 12 oz)

200 g / 7 oz of bacon

8 green apples

500 ml / 1 pint / 2 cups cider

1 onion

1 clove of garlic

1 tbsp olive oil

salt and pepper

SERVES 4 | PREP TIME 40 minutes | COOKING TIME 30 minutes

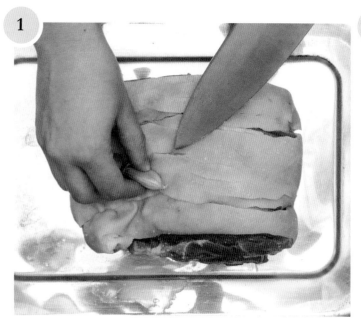

Preheat the oven to 220°C (200° fan) / 425F / gas 7. Place the meat in a baking dish. Pierce with a knife and place the garlic cloves inside the grooves.

Wrap the bacon rashers all the way around it, tucking it into the bottom.

3

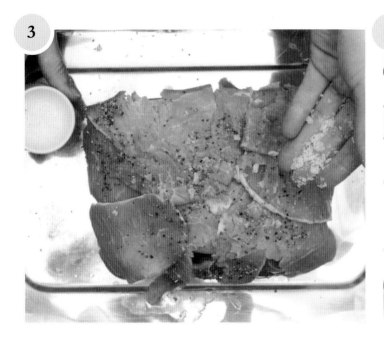

Season with salt and pepper.

4

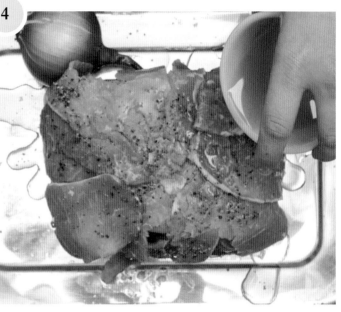

Add the whole onion to the dish and drizzle the meat with olive oil. Bake for 15 minutes.

5

Meanwhile, peel and core the apples. Slice them in half.

6

Add the apples and sprinkle with half of the cider. Put back in the oven for 30 minutes. To serve, cut into slices, arrange the apples around. Drizzle with pan juices and deglaze with the remaining cider. Serve hot.

Leek and Blue Cheese Pie

Ingredients

5 leeks

150 g / 5 oz blue cheese

200 g / 7 oz flour

100 g / 4 oz / 1 stick of butter

250 ml / 9 fl. oz / 1 cup cream

grated nutmeg

salt and pepper

SERVES 4 | PREP TIME 15 minutes | COOKING TIME 40 minutes

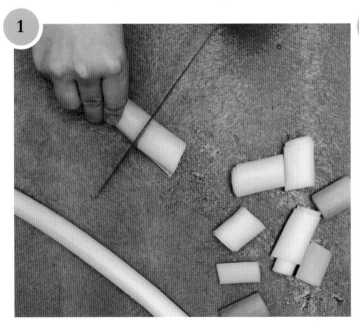

Remove the roots and green parts of the leeks, wash them in cold water. Cut them into three pieces and then in 2 cm / 1" in slices. Steam them for 10 minutes.

Meanwhile, preheat the oven to 220°C (200 fan) / 425F / gas 7. Crumble the blue cheese in a bowl, add the cream, stirring gently.

Season and grate a little nutmeg on top.

Prepare your crumble topping by combining the flour and melted butter with your fingertips to obtain a coarse mixture.

Lightly butter a baking dish, line the bottom with the mixture of blue cheese and cream, then top with the leeks.

Season lightly and place the crumble on top. Bake the in the oven for 30 minutes.

Fish and Chips

Ingredients

1 kg / 2 lb 4 oz cod fillets

1 kg / 2 lb 4 oz potatoes

500 g / 1lb 2 oz garden peas

150 g / 5 oz / 1 cup sifted flour

2 eggs, separated

6 tbsp milk

6 tbsp water

4 tbsp beer

2 tsp sugar

2 lemons

salt

cooking oil (2 l / 4pints)

SERVES 4 | PREP TIME 15 minutes | COOKING TIME 15 minutes

Pour the flour into a bowl, add the sugar and mix.

Make a well in the middle and add the salt, beer and egg yolks.

3

Mix the milk and water together and gradually add to the batter until smooth. Let it chill for 30 minutes in the fridge.

4

Cook the peas in salted boiling water until tender. Cut the potatoes into 2 cm / 1" in chips. Fry in a pan filled with hot oil.

5

Beat the egg whites until stiff and fold into the batter mixture.

6

Rinse the fish cod fillets, dry in a cloth, season and flour. Dip in batter, coat well and cook for 5 minutes in hot oil. Drain on paper towels and serve, with chips, peas and lemon wedges.

Mushroom Risotto

Ingredients

300 g / 11 oz / 1 ½ cup of short grain rice ("Arborio")

250 g / 9 oz of small ceps mushrooms

50 g / 2 oz / ½ stick of butter

1 onion

150 ml / 5 fl. oz / ⅝ cup of white wine

1 l / 1 pint 16 flo. oz / 4 cups of stock

1 tbsp grated Parmesan

2 tbsp cooking oil

1 tsp finely chopped parsley

salt and pepper

SERVES 6 | PREP TIME 30 minutes | COOKING TIME 50 minutes

Prepare and measure all of the ingredients.

Clean the mushrooms and cut them in half.

3

Heat oil in a pan. Sauté mushrooms over high heat for 5 minutes, stirring. Season with salt and pepper and then reserve.

4

Peel and chop the onion. Heat the stock.

5

Melt the butter in a pan. Pour the onion with the rice and fry over low heat, stirring until they become translucent.

6

Then pour in the white wine and season with salt and pepper.

7

8

Cook for about 40 minutes over a low heat, pouring the hot stock spoon by spoon, stirring frequently so the rice does not stick. The liquid should be completely absorbed by the rice while cooking.

When the rice is cooked, add the mushrooms, parsley, a pinch of pepper and very cold butter. Stir and cook for 5 min. Divide into bowls, sprinkle with grated Parmesan and serve immediately.

Vegetable Stroganoff

Ingredients

1 small onion

1 broccoli

2 carrots

pack of green beans

250 g / 9 oz button mushrooms

1 red pepper

200 g / 7 oz / 1 cup uncooked long grain rice

250 ml / 9 fl. oz / 1 cup vegetable stock

2 tbsp sour cream

1 tsp butter

1 tsp hot paprika

2 tsp plain flour

salt

black pepper

Tabasco sauce

SERVES 4 | PREP TIME 20 minutes | COOKING TIME 30 minutes

Finely chop the onion. Cut the pepper into small chunks and slice the mushrooms. Julienne the carrots. Wash the beans and trim the ends.

Cook the green beans in salted boiling water for a few minutes.

Place the carrots in a saucepan and cook in salted boiling water for a few minutes.

Separate the broccoli into small florets and cook in salted boiling water for a few minutes.

Rinse the rice in running water then bring to the boil in a saucepan of salted water and let simmer until cooked through. Drain and reserve. Sweat the onion in butter over medium heat in a high pan.

Add the peppers and mushrooms, let braise for approximately 5 minutes.

Sprinkle with paprika and flour and sauté briefly. Pour the stock into the pan and simmer until the sauce starts to thicken.

Add the broccoli and carrots to the pan.

Season with salt, pepper and Tabasco, then add the green beans.

Coat the vegetables in sour cream. Place the rice on the plate and top with vegetables.

Rice Pudding

Ingredients

200 g / 7 oz / 1 cup short grain rice

900 ml / 1 pint 12 fl. oz / 3 ⅔ cups milk

60 g / 2 ½ oz / ⅓ cup brown sugar

1 vanilla pod

4 pears

150 g / 5 oz / 1 ⅔ cup sugar

1 lemon

1 pinch of cinnamon

SERVES 4 | PREP TIME 15 minutes | COOKING TIME 30 minutes

Using a knife, split the vanilla pod in half and remove the seeds over the milk in a saucepan.

Add the pod and half the brown sugar. Heat the milk but don't bring it to the boil. Filter and reserve the vanilla pod.

3

Rinse the rice and drain. In a saucepan, place 30 ml of vanilla milk and the rice.

4

Cook on a low heat, stirring with a wooden spoon until the milk is absorbed. Gradually add the remaining milk and cook for a total of 25 minutes.

5

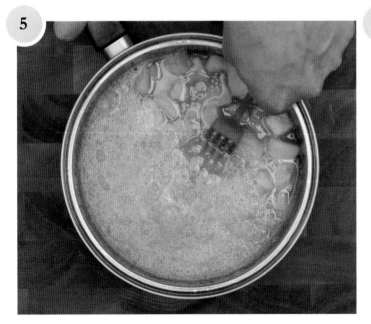

Peel and slice the pears, place them in a saucepan with water and simmer with half the sugar and cinnamon, until tender. Add the lemon juice and crush using a fork to obtain a coarse purée.

6

Once the rice is tender, add the remaining sugar and reserve. Assemble the pudding with the pear puree first then the rice and a pinch of cinnamon and vanilla pod.

Pistachio Panna Cotta

Ingredients

1 l / 1 pint 16 fl. oz / 4 cups of cream

160 g / 5 oz / ⅔ cup of caster sugar

80 g / 3 oz of pistachio paste

3 sheets of gelatine

80 g / 3 oz of whole pistachios

cold water

SERVES 6 | PREP TIME 5 minutes | COOKING TIME 10 minutes

In a saucepan, heat the cream, sugar and pistachio paste to boiling point.

Meanwhile, soak the gelatine leaves in cold water, to soften them without melting.

3

Incorporate the gelatine into the cream (it should melt immediately) and stir gently.

4

Pour the mixture into ramekins and place in the refrigerator. Let them cool for at least 3 hours.

5

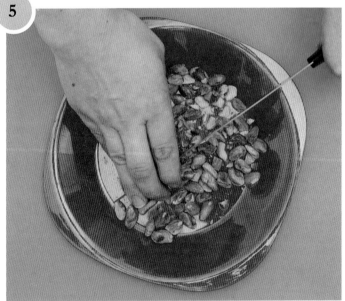

Before serving, chop the pistachios or blend them in a food processor. Unmold the panna cotta and sprinkle the pistachio dust on top.

Chocolate and Almond Tart

Ingredients

For the dough:

125 g / 4 ½ oz / ⅚ plain flour

60 g / 2 ½ oz / ½ stick softened butter

55 g / 2 oz / ½ cup icing sugar

1 egg yolk

1 tbsp semi-skimmed milk

pinch salt

For the ganache:

200 g / 7 oz dark chocolate

150 ml / 5 fl. oz semi-skimmed milk

150 ml / 5 fl. oz cream

1 whole egg

For the topping:

100 g / 4 oz / 1 cup whole almonds

SERVES 2 | PREP TIME 25 minutes | COOKING TIME 20 minutes

Pre heat the oven to 160°C (140° fan) / 300F / gas 2. Mix the flour and icing sugar in a bowl. Add one egg yolk and butter at room temperature.

Work the dough by hand, until it's crumbly. Add a little milk to avoid the dough breaking.

Spread the dough using a rolling pin. Line the tin with the pastry, cutting off any excess. Blind bake, covered with a baking sheet and dried beans or rice for 10 minutes.

Boil the milk and cream in a saucepan, pour in the chocolate pieces and mix thoroughly. Add the egg and mix again.

Add half of the chopped almonds to the mix, keeping the other half for the top of the tart.

Pour the mix into the pastry case. Bake at 150°C (130° fan) / 290F / gas 2, for 10 minutes. Sprinkle with the remaining almonds and allow to cool to room temperature before serving.

Chocolate and Mint Mousse

Ingredients

350 g / 12 oz dark chocolate

100 g / 4 oz / ½ cup caster sugar

75 g / 3 oz / ⅔ stick butter, softened

4 whole eggs

1 tsp mint extract or mint syrup

fresh mint leaves

pinch of salt

SERVES 3 | PREP TIME 15 minutes | COOKING TIME 3 hours

Melt the chocolate in a Bain Marie, mixing well.

Add the caster sugar and softened butter to the Bain Marie. Mix well using a wooden spoon.

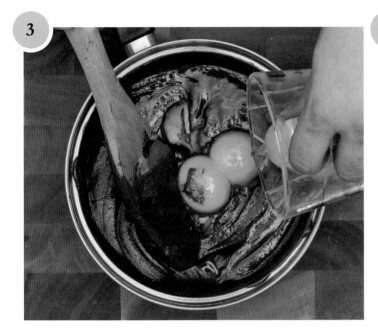

Break the eggs, add the yolks to the chocolate mixture and blend.

Add a pinch of salt to the egg whites and beat until stiff. Fold the whites gently in the chocolate mixture.

Add 1 tsp of mint extract or mint syrup and blend gently.

Place the mixture in the serving dishes and place in the refrigerator for 3 hours. Decorate with fresh mint leaves and serve.

Strawberry Charlotte

Ingredients

500 g / 1lb 2 oz fresh strawberries

300 g / 11 oz finger biscuit

75 g / 3 oz / ⅔ powdered sugar

3 tbsp of strawberry or lemon syrup

250 ml / 9 fl. oz / 1 cup of crème fraiche

2 tbsp rum (optional)

fresh mint leaves and icing sugar, for decoration

SERVES 6 | PREP TIME 20 minutes | COOKING TIME 3 hours

Wash the strawberries under cold water, hull them and slice them in half.

Mix them with sugar in a bowl. Reserve a handful for decoration.

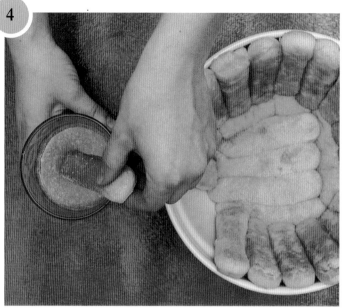

Add the cream to the strawberries and and mix gently in a dish.

Mix the syrup in a glass of water (add the rum if you like). Quickly dip the biscuits in the syrup, one by one. They should not be completely soaked, just wet. Arrange them in a mould.

Pour the strawberries and cream on the biscuit bed.

Cover with another layer of biscuits. Place the bottom of a small plate onto the charlotte to settle the ingredients, pressing down lightly. Place it in the refrigerator for 3 hours. To serve, place it onto a plate and decorate with strawberries and mint leaves.

Tiramisu

Ingredients

400 g / 14 oz finger biscuits

250 g / 9 oz / 2 cups ground coffee

50 g / 2 oz / ⅓ cup cocoa powder

500 ml / 18 fl. oz / 2 cups double cream

200 ml / 7 fl. oz / ⅘ cup cane sugar syrup

150 ml / 5 fl. oz almond liqueur

75 g / 3 oz of icing sugar

500 ml / 18 fl. oz / 2 cups of hot water

SERVES 6 | PREP TIME 15 minutes | COOKING TIME 60-70 minutes

Prepare and measure all of the ingredients. Boil the water for the coffee.

Prepare the coffee by passing the hot water over the coffee.

3

Add the cane sugar syrup and almond liqueur. Mix well.

4

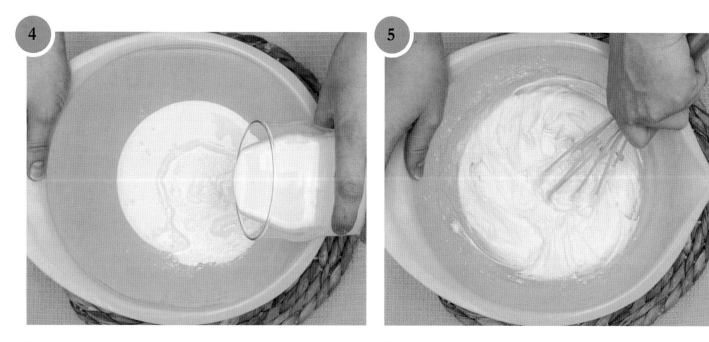

Pour the cream and icing sugar into a bowl.

5

Whisk for 10 minutes to obtain a stiff whipped cream.

6

Quickly dip the biscuits in the coffee mixture.

7

Arrange the biscuits by crumbling them and laying them in the serving cups.

8

Spread a layer of whipped cream on the biscuits. Repeat the process a couple of times to form layers. Chill for at least 6 hours. Sprinkle with cocoa and serve.

Chocolate Truffles

Ingredients

300 g / 11 oz dark chocolate

100 g / 4 oz / 1 stick butter

2 egg yolks

125 g / 4 ½ oz / 1 cup icing sugar

1 tsp milk

40 ml / 3 tbsp cream

cocoa powder for coating

MAKES 20 | PREP TIME 10 minutes | COOKING TIME 10 minutes

Prepare and measure all of the ingredients. Break the chocolate into small pieces.

Place the chocolate pieces to a small pan.

3

Add the milk and melt over a low heat. Mix with a wooden spoon until mixture is smooth.

4

Add the butter in small chunks, whilst mixing continuously.

5

Add the egg yolks one at a time, blending well after each addition.

6

Finally, add the cream. Mix well using a wooden spoon.

7

Add the sugar, beating continuously, ensuring the mixture is blended well.

8

Pour the mixture into a bowl and place in the fridge for at least 2 hours.

9

When the mixture is cool and hard, form small balls the size of walnuts and place to one side.

10

Roll the ball in the cocoa powder, dusting off any excess. Keep refrigerated until serving time.

Crêpes Suzette

Ingredients

250 g / 9 oz / 1 ⅔ cups plain flour

100 g / 4 oz / 1 stick butter

4 eggs

1 tbsp vanilla sugar

500 ml / 18 fl. oz / 2 cups cold milk

60 g / 2 ½ oz / ¼ cup sugar

grated zest of 2 oranges

pinch of salt

splash of brandy

SERVES 6 | PREP TIME 45 minutes | COOKING TIME 15 minutes

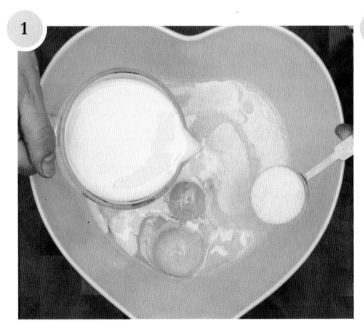

To prepare the batter, mix the flour, eggs, 1 tbsp of vanilla sugar, a pinch of salt and cold milk in a bowl until the consistency is smooth.

Whisk well for a few minutes. If the batter is too thick, add a little milk, it should be of coating consistency.

3

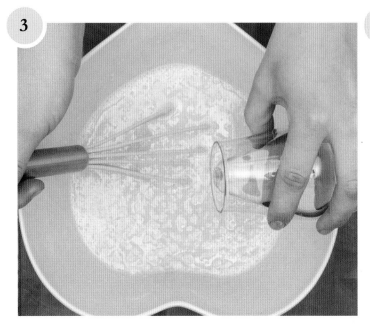

Add half of the melted butter and a dash of brandy to the mix.

4

To cook the pancakes, wipe the bottom of a hot pan with oil or butter. Add the batter mix to the pan and swirl the pan so that all of the mix spreads out.

5

In a bowl, mix the rest of the butter with the sugar into a creamy paste, add the grated zest of 1 ½ oranges, and some drops of brandy.

6

Spread this mixture on each pancake and fold them in half. Decorate with the rest of the orange zest.

Bread and Butter Pudding

Ingredients

250 g / 9 oz of brioche (or plain bread without crust)

100 g / 4 oz / 1 stick of butter, softened

2 eggs

50 g / 2 oz / ¼ cup of sugar

½ teaspoon cinnamon

50 g / 2 oz ¼ cup of raisins soaked in rum

55 g / 2 oz / ⅓ cup brown sugar

250 ml / 9 fl. oz / 1 cup of milk

250 ml / 9 fl. oz / 1 cup of cream

SERVES 4 | PREP TIME 15 minutes | COOKING TIME 30 minutes

Preheat the oven to 180°C (160° fan) / 350F / gas 4. Cut the brioche/bread into thin slices and butter them.

Arrange the slices on the oven dish, drizzling the drained raisins on each slice.

154

Beat the eggs, then add the sugar and cinnamon and keep beating with a whisk for a few minutes.

Add the milk and keep beating with a whisk before finally adding the cream.

Pour the mixture over the brioche/bread and let it absorb for a few minutes.

Sprinkle with brown sugar. Bake for 30 minutes until golden. Serve with custard, ice cream or fresh fruits.

Bakewell Tart

Ingredients

For the tart:

200 g / 7 oz / 1 ⅓ cups plain flour

100 g / 4 oz / 1 stick of cold butter, diced

40 g / 1 ½ oz / ⅓ cup icing sugar

1 small egg, beaten

pinch of salt

For the filling:

300 g / 11 oz raspberry jam

200 g / 7 oz / 1 ⅓ cups of whole almonds

130 g / 4 ½ oz / 1 ¼ stick of butter

120 g / 4 ½ oz / ½ cup of sugar

50 g / 2 oz / ½ cup of flaked almonds

3 eggs

SERVES 8 | PREP TIME 20 minutes | COOKING TIME 45 minutes

Butter and flour the pan. To prepare the dough sift together the flour and icing sugar.

Add the diced, cold butter and work into the flour and sugar using your fingertips until the mixture resembles fine breadcrumbs.

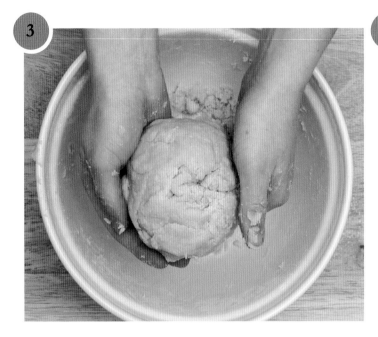

Add the salt and beaten egg, working by hand until forming a ball, film and refrigerate for 30 minutes.

Chop the whole almonds finely. Meanwhile, whisk the butter and sugar until the mixture becomes creamy. Add the eggs and the almonds, and whisk. Reserve.

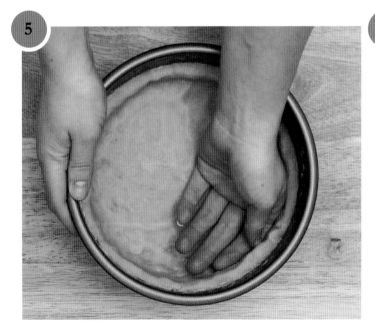

Spread the dough on a floured surface and line the mould with it. Refrigerate for 1 hour. Blind bake the pastry covered in foil and weighted down with rice or beans for 10 minutes in a preheated oven at 180°C (160° fan) / 350F / gas 4. Remove from the oven.

Let it cool a few minutes then pour over the raspberry jam and smooth. Spread the almond mix, and sprinkle with almonds. Bake for 35 minutes. Cool completely before serving.

Raspberry Trifle

Ingredients

250 g / 9 oz / 2 cups raspberries

200 g / 7 oz / 1 ⅓ cups of mascarpone cheese

3 tbsp sugar

juice of 2 lemons

4 shortbread or cinnamon biscuits

For the Custard:

4 egg yolks

50 ml / 2 fl. oz / ⅕ cup of milk

60 g / 2 ½ oz / ¼ cup of sugar

1 pack of vanilla sugar

SERVES 4 | PREP TIME 20 minutes | COOKING TIME 10 minutes

To prepare the custard, mix the egg yolks and sugar in a saucepan, until the mixture is frothy.

Add the cold milk and place on a medium heat, stirring constantly.

When the mixture coats the spoon, and before boiling point, remove from the heat and plunge the saucepan into cold water to stop the cooking.

In a bowl, mix the mascarpone cheese with the sugar and lemon juice.

Crush the biscuits and spread half of the mix into 4 glasses.

Add the mascarpone, raspberries and custard. Repeat this process ending with mascarpone. Decorate with a round of raspberries and a drop of custard. Garnish with chocolate decorations. Chill for 2 hours before serving.

Chocolate Cheesecake

Ingredients

280 g / 10 oz / 1 ⅝ cup digestive biscuits

250 g / 9 oz / 1 ⅔ cups ricotta cheese

100 g / 4 oz / ½ cup cream cheese

80 g / 3 oz dark chocolate

60 g 2 ½ oz / ½ stick butter, melted, warmed

75 g / 3 oz / ⅔ cup icing sugar

30 g / 2 tbsp powdered sugar

1 packet vanilla sugar

3 egg whites

cocoa powder for decoration

SERVES 6 | PREP TIME 25 minutes | COOKING TIME 40 minutes

Preheat the oven to 150°C (130° fan) / 300F / gas 2. Prepare and measure all of the ingredients.

Mix the biscuits coarsely, melt the butter and add to the biscuits until you obtain a smooth paste.

Spread the mixture at the bottom and sides of a cake tin using a wooden spoon.

Drain the cream cheese, then mix with the Ricotta using a whisk.

Beat the egg whites until stiff with 10 g / ½ oz of granulated sugar.

Break the chocolate into pieces and melt it in a bowl over a Bain Marie or in the microwave (be careful not to cook/burn it).

7

In a bowl mix the chocolate, icing sugar, vanilla sugar and remaining caster sugar.

8

Incorporate this mixture to the egg whites folding it very gently.

9

Add the cheese mix to the bowl and stri well.

10

Pour the mixture into the pastry tin, and bake for 30 minutes. Remove from the oven and allow to cool completely before dusting with cocoa powder and serving.

Eton Mess

Ingredients

For the meringue:

4 egg whites

225 g / 8 oz / 1 cup caster sugar

1 tsp corn flour

1 tsp vanilla extract

1 tsp white wine vinegar

For the dessert:

350 g / 12 oz fresh berries

250 ml / 9 fl. oz / 1 cup whipping cream

50 g / 2 oz / ¼ cup vanilla sugar

100 g / 4 oz / ½ cup caster sugar

250 g / 9 oz mascarpone cheese

icing sugar for decoration

SERVES 6 | PREP TIME 15 minutes | COOKING TIME 20 minutes

Prepare and measure all of the ingredients. Wash the berries.

Pre-heat the oven to 180°C (160° fan) / 350F / gas 4. Prepare a baking tray by lining it with baking paper.

3

For the meringue, beat the egg whites with an electric mixer or by hand until they stiffen, then, gradually add the sugar and keeping whisking.

4

Mix the white wine vinegar, corn flour and vanilla extract together, in a small bowl.

5

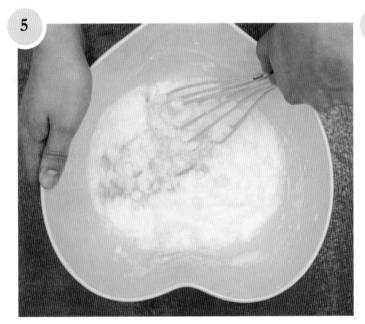

Incorporate the vinegar mixture to the meringue mixture and blend using a whisk.

6

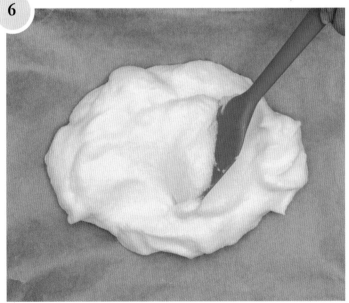

Spread the mixture on your tray evenly and bake in the oven for 15 minutes until the top is slightly golden but the consistency is still a bit bouncy.

Remove from the oven and reserve. Mix the mascarpone and the caster sugar together. In a separate bowl, mix the cream and vanilla sugar together.

Crush the meringue using the end of a rolling pin, into uneven pieces.

Top with the cream and mascarpone mix, and combine.

Finally, add the berries. Serve immediately so that the meringue doesn't get too chewy. You can sprinkle icing sugar on top for decoration.

Chocolate Fondue

Ingredients

200 g / 7 oz dark chocolate

100 g / 4 oz / ½ cup sugar

100 g / 4 oz / 1 stick butter

5 eggs

2 tbsp flour

oil and flour for pan

For the Custard:

4 egg yolks

50 ml / 2 fl. oz / ⅕ cup of milk

60 g / 2 ½ oz / ¼ cup of sugar

1 packet of vanilla sugar

SERVES 8 | PREP TIME 15 minutes | COOKING TIME 20 minutes

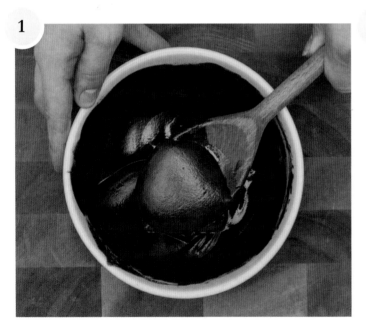

Preheat the oven to 190°C (170° fan) / 375F / gas 5. Put the chocolate in a bowl with 4 tbsp of water, place in the microwave for 50 seconds, checking constantly, until melted.

Add the butter to the chocolate, then the sugar. Wait a few minutes as the mixture shouldn't be too hot.

3

Incorporate the eggs one by one, mixing with a wooden spoon. Stir in the flour, 1 tablespoon at a time while still mixing.

4

Oil some small ramekins and sprinkle with flour. Pour the mixture in. Bake for 15 to 20 minutes depending on your oven.

5

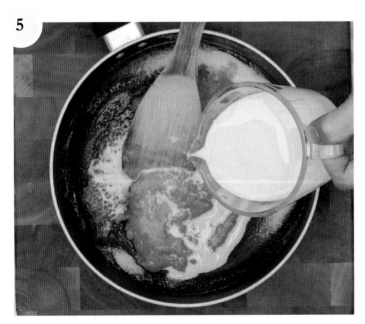

In a saucepan, mix the egg yolks and sugar until the mixture is frothy. Add the cold milk. Put on the stove and heat, stirring constantly.

6

When the mixture coats the spoon, remove from the heat and plunge the pan into cold water to stop it cooking. Let it cool and unmould the ramekins. Slice the top of the cakes so that the centre appears and serve with custard.

Profiteroles

Ingredients

For the choux pastry:

150 g / 5 oz / 1 cup of flour

4 eggs

110 g / 4 oz / 1 stick butter

1 tbsp of sugar

pinch of salt

For the filling and topping:

500 ml / 18 fl. oz / 2 cups vanilla ice cream

150 g / 5 oz / 1 cup dark chocolate

30 g / 1 oz / ¼ stick butter

1 tbsp milk

SERVES 6 | PREP TIME 45 minutes | COOKING TIME 40 minutes

1

Preheat the oven to 220°C (200° fan) / 425F / gas 7. Cut the butter into small pieces. Place in a pan with the sugar, salt and 200 ml of water. Gently heat.

2

Remove from the heat and add the flour all at once, whisking. Return to the heat and cook, stirring quickly until the dough pulls away from pan. Do not over beat.

3

Remove the pan from the heat and stir in the eggs one at a time, beating constantly. Put the dough into a piping bag fitted with a straight-sided tip.

4

Pipe small balls of dough on a baking sheet, spacing them well apart. Bake for 20-25 minutes, leaving the door slightly open to let the moisture escape. Remove from the oven and let cool.

5

Break the chocolate in a saucepan. Add the butter and milk. Melt over a low heat, stirring until you obtain a sauce. Reserve in a water bath.

6

Slice the top off of the choux balls. Fill each with a small scoop of ice cream. Place the caps on top. Place the choux balls in bowls and drizzle with hot chocolate sauce. Serve immediately.

Lemon sorbet

Ingredients

Juice and zest of 2 lemons

450 ml / 16 fl. oz / 1 ⅘ cups water

140 g / 5 oz / ⅔ cups of sugar

2 egg whites

SERVES 4 | PREP TIME 10 minutes | COOKING TIME 20 minutes

Juice the lemons and grate the zest from one of them.

Prepare the syrup by adding the sugar to the water and gently heating, until the sugar has melted. Reduce slightly and let it cool.

3

Mix the lemon juice, zest and syrup together in a bowl. Once blended, pour into an ice box and freeze.

4

After 3 hours, pour the mixture back into a bowl and beat to make it fluffy.

5

Finally, add the egg whites and freeze again for at least 3 hours. Serve the sorbet with grated lemon zest on top.

Cheesecake

Ingredients

250 g / 9 oz cinnamon biscuits

150 g / 5 oz digestive biscuits

110 g / 4 oz / 1 stick of soft unsalted butter

450 g / 1 lb / 2 cups cream cheese

250 g / 9 oz / 2 cups Ricotta / cottage cheese

200 ml / 7 fl. oz / $\frac{4}{5}$ cup double cream

150 g / 5 oz / $\frac{2}{3}$ cup vanilla sugar

3 eggs

2 egg yolks

1 tbsp of corn flour

red fruit coulis

berries for decoration

SERVES 8 | PREP TIME 30 minutes | COOKING TIME 90 minutes

1

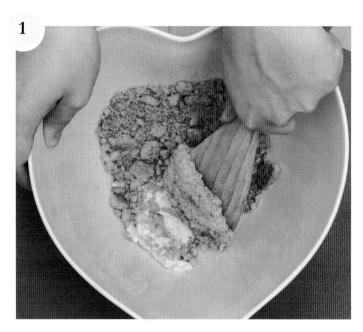

Preheat the over to 180°C (160° fan) / 350F / gas 4. Crush all the biscuits to a powder, add the softened butter and continue mixing.

2

In a 30 cm / 12" in dish (lined with parchment paper), spread the mixture on the bottom going up a little on the side.

3

Bake the biscuit for 8 minutes in the oven and let cool. Reduce the oven to 150°C . Whip the 2 cheeses with the sugar for 1 minute.

4

Add the whole eggs and yolks one by one. Add the cream, cornstarch and whisk for a few minutes.

5

Pour half this mixture over the biscuit dough. Drizzle red fruit coulis over the cheese mix.

6

Then pour the rest of the cheese mix on top very gently, trying not to disturb the coulis. Bake for 90 minutes at the reduced temperature. Let it cool then put in the fridge for 6 hours. Drizzle with the rest of the red fruit coulis and add some berries for decoration.

Chocolate Sundae

Ingredients

150 g / 5 oz milk chocolate

100 g / 4 oz dark chocolate

2 eggs

1 egg yolk

2 tbsp icing sugar

40 ml / 1 ½ fl. oz / 3 tbsp of whisky

2 tsp grated orange rind

400 ml / 14 fl. oz / 1 ⅔ cups double cream

coloured sprinkles, for decoration

SERVES 6 | PREP TIME 15 minutes | COOKING TIME 30 minutes

Break the chocolate into pieces and melt it in a bowl over a Bain Marie.

Beat the egg yolks with the sugar in a bowl until frothy. Add the melted chocolate and mix.

3

Add the whisky and orange zest and let it cool slightly. Beat the cream until stiff and do the same with the 2 egg whites.

4

Mix the egg whites gently with the cooled chocolate mixture. Place ⅔ of this mixture in the fridge to set.

5

Combine the rest of the chocolate mixture with the whipped cream and place in the fridge to set as well.

6

Put the dark mousse into the glass first, then top with the milk chocolate mousse preferably with a piping bag. Refrigerate again before serving or place in the freezer, for a real frozen taste. Top with coloured sprinkles and decorate as you like.

Lemon Meringue Pie

Ingredients

For the dough :

250 g / 9 oz / 1 ⅔ cups plain flour

1 pack of vanilla sugar

1 egg

pinch of salt

125 g / 4 ½ oz / 1 ⅙ stick softened butter

For the lemon Cream:

5 egg yolks

3 egg whites

1 tbsp cornstarch

75 ml / 3 fl. oz / ⅓ cup cream

125 g / 4 ½ oz / 1 cup icing sugar

100 ml / 4 fl. oz / ⅖ cup lemon juice

1 tsp lemon zest, grated

For the meringue:

3 egg whites

125 g / 4 ½ oz / 1 cup icing sugar

1 tsp lemon zest, grated

SERVES 8 | PREP TIME 25 minutes | COOKING TIME 35 minutes

Prepare and measure all of the ingredients.

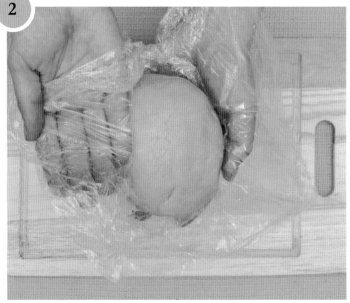

Prepare the pastry by mixing all of the ingredients by hand or in a food processor. Wrap in plastic and rest for 1 hour in the fridge.

3

Pre-heat the oven to 200°C (180° fan) / 400F / gas 6. Flatten the dough to 5mm / ¼ inch thick. Butter the tart mould and line with the pastry.

4

Place a baking sheet on to the pastry and dry beans or rice. Blind bake for 10 minutes. Remove the baking sheet and beans/rice and let the pastry case cool down.

5

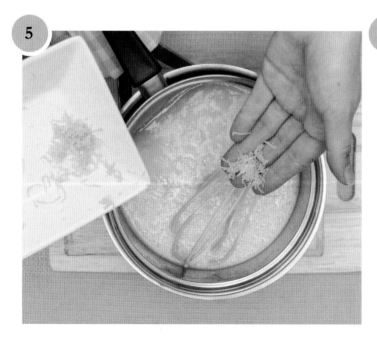

For the lemon cream, beat the egg yolks with the cornflour, cream and half the icing sugar over a bain-marie. Add the juice and lemon zest to the mixture.

6

Beat the egg whites until stiff, incorporating the remaining icing sugar and then fold the egg whites to the lemon mixture.

7

Pour the cream on the chilled pastry case and bake for 25 minutes in the middle of the oven at 150°C (130° fan) / 300F / gas 2. Allow to cool.

8

For the meringue, beat the egg whites until stiff, then add the icing sugar gradually.

9

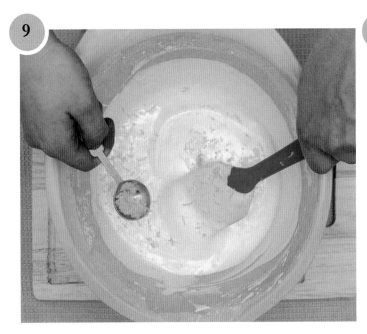

Gently fold the lemon zest into the meringue mixture.

10

Cover the tart with the egg whites and form a decorative shape (or you can use a piping bag. Bake at 240°C (220° fan) / 475F / gas 9 until the meringue is just starting to brown.

Black Forest Gateau

Ingredients

200 g / 7 oz dark chocolate (patisserie)

500 g / 1 lb 2oz cherries (fresh or in syrup)

110 ml / 4 fl. oz / ½ cup cherry liqueur

6 eggs

400 ml / 14 fl. oz / 1 ⅔ cups whipping cream

200 g / 7 oz / 1 cup caster sugar

100 g / 4oz / 1 stick butter, melted, warmed

75 g / 3 oz / ⅔ cup ground almonds

100 g / 4 oz / ⅔ cup cocoa powder

50 g / 2 oz / ⅓ cup flour

1 tsp baking powder

3 packs of vanilla sugar

30 g / 1 oz / 2 tbsp icing sugar

SERVES 4 | PREP TIME 60 minutes | COOKING TIME 30 minutes

Prepare and measure all of the ingredients. Using a vegetable peeler, make chocolate shavings out of the chocolate. Reserve.

Pour the cherries in a bowl, let them macerate in cherry liqueur for 2 hours in advance then drain them and keep the juice. Preheat the oven to 180°C (160° fan) / 350F / gas 4.

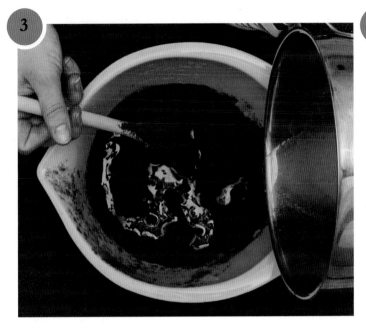

Place the cream in the refrigerator. In a bowl, place the egg yolks, ¼ of the sugar, the melted butter, almonds, cocoa, and mix well.

Add the sifted flour and baking powder and 1 tablespoon of vanilla sugar.

Mix to a smooth paste. Beat the egg whites until stiff, adding a pinch of salt. Fold them gently into the dough.

Pour the batter into three moulds of the same diameter, greased and floured and bake for 20 minutes. Unmuold and let cool on a rack.

Make a syrup with the remaining sugar, 1 packet of vanilla sugar and 250 ml / 9 fl. oz / 1 cup of water.

Remove from the heat and add the juice from the macerated cherries. Pour onto the three baked cakes and leave it to soak in.

Pour the cream into a bowl. Beat using a whisk, slowly and gradually increasing speed. When the cream has changed consistency, gently add the icing sugar and the last pack of vanilla sugar.

To assemble, spread ¼ of whipped cream on one cake and cover with cherries. Place a second cake on top and repeat. Add the third cake and cover with cream and chocolate shavings. Place in the refrigerator for 3 hours before serving.

Chocolate Brownie

Ingredients

120 g / 4 ½ oz dark patisserie chocolate

110 g / 4 oz / 1 stick soft butter

butter for pan

55 g / 2 oz / ⅓ cup plain flour

2 eggs

110 g / 4 oz / ½ cup caster sugar

1 tsp vanilla extract

10 fudge pieces with salted butter

12 white chocolate squares (about 125 g / 4 ½ oz)

SERVES 8-10 | PREP TIME 20 minutes | COOKING TIME 25 minutes

1	2

Preheat the oven to 180°C (160° fan) / 350F / gas 4. Melt the chocolate and butter in a bowl placed on a Bain Marie.

Grease the square/rectangle pan and line the bottom with a little flour and shake out the excess.

3

Cut the squares of white chocolate and fudge into small pieces. Beat the eggs with the sugar and vanilla extract until frothy.

4

Pour in the melted chocolate, then the sifted flour.

5

Add the cubes of caramel and white chocolate chunks.

6

Mix well and pour into the tray. Cook in the oven for 20 to 25 minutes. Slice into cubes and serve warm.

Banoffee Pie

Ingredients

150 g / 5 oz / 1 ½ cups digestive biscuits

150 g / 5 oz / 1 ½ cups flaked almonds

75 g / 3 oz ⅔ stick butter, melted

400 ml / 14 fl. oz / 1 ⅔ cups condensed milk

4 bananas

75o ml / 1 pint 6 fl. oz / 3 cups double cream, chilled

1 tbsp icing sugar

unsweetened cocoa nibs for decoration

SERVES 6 | PREP TIME 20 minutes | COOKING TIME 1 hour

A few hours in advance, prepare the Dulce de Leche (milk jam). Place the condensed milk, still in its jar, in a pressure cooker and cover ¾ of the way with water. Cook for 45 minutes, until the first whistle. Do not open the jar until it has cooled down completely.

Break the biscuits into pieces and blend into crumbs. Add the melted butter, mix, then line the bottom of a buttered round dish and smooth the surface with the back of a tablespoon. Refrigerate for ½ hour to fully solidify the base.

3

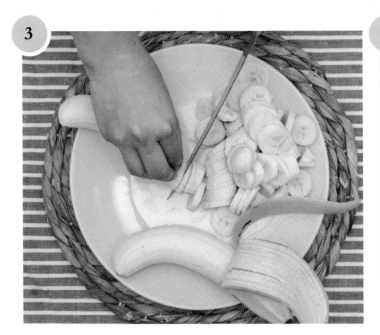

Slice the bananas, and simmer to soften them.

4

Beat the cream using a whisk, adding the icing sugar, until the cream stiffens. Do not whisk too much or the cream will turn into butter. Pour half of the cream into the dish and spread with the back of a spoon.

5

Sprinkle half of the banana on the cream, then half the Dulce de Leche, the rest of the cream except for 2 tbsp for decoration, and the rest of the banana slices.

6

Cover the cake with the rest of the Dulce de Leche and decorate using a fork. Chill for at least 1 hour. Decorate with blobs of whipped cream sprinkled with cocoa nibs and use sliced almonds to decorate the sides of the cake.

Lemon Drizzle Cake

Ingredients

For the cake:

115 g / 4 oz / 1 stick butter, softened

115 g / 4 oz / ½ cup caster sugar

125 g / 4 oz ½ / ⅝ cup self-raising flour

4 large eggs

180 g / 6 oz / 1 ½ cup ground almonds

zest and juice of 2 lemons

For the syrup:

100 g / 4 oz / ½ cup sugar

juice of 1 lemon

SERVES 6 | PREP TIME 20 minutes | COOKING TIME 45 minutes

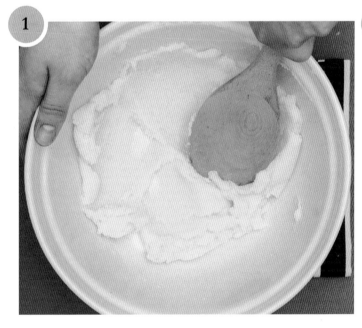

Pre-heat the oven to 180°C (160° fan) / 350F / gas 4, and grease/flour a cake mould. Using a wooden spoon, beat the butter and sugar together until creamy.

Add the eggs one at a time, mixing well after each addition.

Add the ground almonds, lemon zest, lemon juice and flour.

Pour the mixture into the mould and bake for 40 minutes, then remove and let it cool on a wire rack.

Prepare the syrup by mixing the sugar and lemon juice in a small saucepan over a low heat, stirring until the sugar dissolves. The syrup should not be too thick.

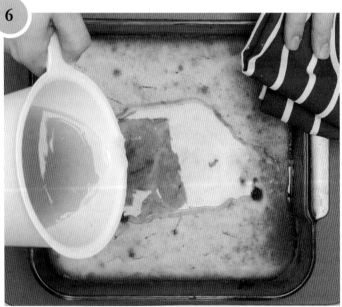

While the cake is still hot, make small holes using a toothpick and pour half of the syrup over the entire cake. Let the syrup cool and mix with icing sugar to pipe decorations on the cake.

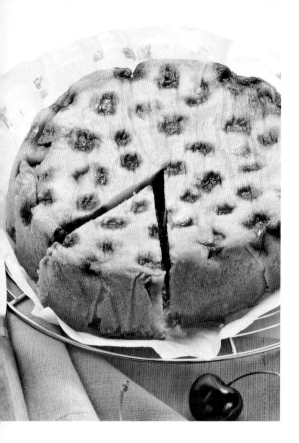

Cherry Clafoutis

Ingredients

500 g / 1 lb 2 oz fresh cherries

50 g / 2 oz / ⅓ cup plain flour

30 ml / 1 fl. oz / 2 tbsp milk

120 g / 4 ½ oz / ½ cup of caster sugar

6 eggs

SERVES 6 | PREP TIME 15 minutes | COOKING TIME 35 minutes

Preheat the oven to 150°C (130° fan) / 300F / gas 2. Rinse the cherries, hull them and remove the stones.

Pour ¾ of the sugar in a bowl and add the eggs. Beat using a whisk, until frothy.

Add the flour, one spoonful at a time whilst whisking constantly.

Then add the milk to the mixture and beat again.

Arrange the cherries in a round buttered pie dish.

Pour the mix into the dish. Bake for 35 minutes. When it is cooked, let it cool for 5 minutes then sprinkle the remaining sugar on top.

Index